JUST: IMAGINE

THE SOCIAL JUSTICE AWAKENING

DANIELLE **STRICKLAND**
CAMPBELL **ROBERTS**

Authentic

MILTON KEYNES • COLORADO SPRINGS • HYDERABAD

SPRING HARVEST
Equipping the Church for action

15 14 13 12 11 10 09 7 6 5 4 3 2 1

First published 2009 by Spring Harvest Publishing Division and Authentic Media
9 Holdom Avenue, Bletchley, Milton Keynes, Bucks, MK1 1QR, UK
1820 Jet Stream Drive, Colorado Springs, CO 80921, USA
OM Authentic Media, Medchal Road, Jeedimetla
Village, Secunderabad 500 055, A.P., India
www.authenticmedia.co.uk

Authentic Media is a division of IBS-STL U.K., limited by guarantee, with
its Registered Office at Kingstown Broadway, Carlisle, Cumbria CA3 0HA.
Registered in England & Wales No. 1216232. Registered charity 270162

British Library Cataloguing in Publication Data

A catalogue record for this book is available from the British Library

ISBN-13: 978-1-85078-841-6

Cover design by Suzi Perkins
Typesetting and layout by Perri Winter
Set in Hoefler Text and Helvetica Ultralight
Print Management by Adare
Printed and bound in the UK by J F Print Ltd., Sparkford, Somerset

JUST: **IMAGINE**

THE SOCIAL JUSTICE AGENDA

CONTENTS

001 **Preface:** The Journey Begins

009 **One:** More Than A Dream

015 **Section One: Foundations of Justice**

017 **Two:** Biblical Justice

033 **Three:** Salvationist Foundations

043 **Section Two: Acting Justly**

045 **Four:** Global Community

061 **Five:** The Three Justices

087 **Section Three: Let Justice Roll**

089 **Six:** Imagining a Better World

099 **Seven:** Prophetic Response

113 **Eight:** Political Response

123 **Nine:** Practical Response

135 **Conclusion:** Live the Dream

139 **Justice Resources**

142 **Books**

144 **Endnotes**

THE JOURNEY BEGINS

THE JOURNEY BEGINS

This book is in three sections; each of which contains chapters followed by excerpts of speeches and articles. It may help to read the sections in a group for discussion. The material is a mixture of introduction and exploration – we encourage you to take your time and try to incorporate the ideas into your experience. Our hope is that social justice won't be something that simply informs your mind – but radically alters your life.

This book has been written by two Christians who imagine a better world. Both authors recognize that our position in this social justice perspective is heavily influenced by Western world experience. We hope, though, that the tools we've accumulated throughout the journey will be transferable and helpful to anyone, from anywhere, who is committed to joining the dreamers of a new world, and that these tools will aid you in a commitment to fight injustice for the long haul.

The start of our journeys towards justice went like this:

Danielle Strickland

My first 'mission trip' was to Malawi, Africa in the summer of 1989. Along with a bunch of middle-class Western teenagers I went to discover and change the world. And I did. Africa didn't change much (all I left behind were some clothes, a few newly built brick classrooms attached to a church, and one dead, fat, hairy spider)[1] but I did change the world. After that trip, 'my world' began to take on new meaning and greater depth. Gone were the feel-good days of comfortable, personal salvation; I had now entered a dangerous world of poverty, inequality and social responsibility. When I overate, I didn't just feel overfed, I felt like something was wrong with how the world operated, and fully understood that I was implicated in it.

I remember baby Joshua, who was born one week and died of malnutrition the next. Somehow, even though thousands of miles separated us and our situations were vastly different, I felt connected. That connection is the key to world-changing behaviour. It is about a life no longer content with the 'inevitable' systems of oppression. Cycles of poverty and systemic global injustice must stop, and we are living in an unprecedented age in which they can stop. We hold the power of wealth, intellect, resources and a will to change the world, not just talk about it. Sure, it will start with our individual world (and needs to) but it won't end there. This spirit, a global-transforming resolve, will adjust the way we see the world and how we contribute to it.

My first look at injustice on a global scale was a quick and rough glimpse into the bigger picture. But it left me hungry to understand and uncomfortable with the status quo. As I entered a new world of discovery and challenge I slowly began to emerge out of the land of pessimistic prophetic judgement[2] and mature into a world of new possibilities. My heart echoed the cry of a whole generation choosing to believe that we could make poverty history!

Years later I found myself in Canada's poorest area, the downtown eastside of Vancouver, praying Psalm 97 over the neighbourhood. As I prayed, the Lord began to challenge me with verse eight, the righteous are 'glad at the judgements of the Lord.' I was convicted as I tried to recall a time in my life when I had rejoiced at the Lord's judgement. In fact, it was the opposite. When I think of the judgement of God I think 'hide' and resonate with that bumper sticker that says, 'Jesus is coming. Quick, look busy!' I realized that the majority of people who rejoice at justice are those who have been oppressed. When a righteous judge comes to rule it is good news for people who have been exploited and abused by unjust systems. That's when I understood that I needed not only to *help* the poor but actually position myself *with* the poor. *I want to be on the side of justice.* I want to be at the party at the end of all time when justice will flourish and the majority of the world will be celebrating liberation, equality and bounty. I decided to realign my life alongside the Word of God.

Now, after years of working with people, systems and communities, the proverbial penny has dropped – social justice is a complex issue. Most of what we see wrong with the world seems as though it should be easy to fix. In reality, when we begin to work with individuals we quickly grasp that the vice called injustice has a fierce grip. Multiply that by millions (even billions) and it's obvious that we have a huge struggle ahead of us.

Visiting my friend Annie, a drug addict who struggled with a severe mental illness, in a psychiatric hospital one day, I had a further revelation. She looked at me with a big smile as I approached her and said, 'It sure must feel good to fulfil Jesus' words in Matthew; you must feel blessed.' Annie understood that the blessing of the visit was for me, not for her. She knew she was blessed and had the keys to the Kingdom. There is a strong smell of social justice in this. Isaiah 58 suggests that our healing will come as we get on with the work of justice. Fighting injustice (as we will discover) is not so much about bringing 'liberation' to those who are poor and broken – it's often about allowing the Kingdom to bring liberation to both the oppressor and the oppressed. It is the radical transformation of the Kingdom of God that Martin Luther King Jr. spoke about in his 'I have a dream' speech at the Lincoln memorial in Washington, DC that infamous day.[3] His dream wasn't about the oppressed rising in power, but of the oppressor laying down his rule and the oppressed laying down his hurt and both of them holding hands, joining together. This is a Kingdom idea of social justice. At his inauguration celebration as the new president of South Africa, Nelson Mandela invited his jailer to sit at his table of honour, no longer an enemy but a friend. This kind of kingdom is not simply a judgement or the overthrow of a system, but the solution to the problem of injustice itself.

What stirs me most these days is a community of people called 'the church' who were born for this fight. General William Booth of The Salvation Army (a social reform movement started in the UK) said it like this, 'Without excuse and self-consideration of health or limb or life, true soldiers fight, live to fight, love the thickest of the fight, and die in the midst of it.'[4] I can only imagine what God's plans are for a body like ours. Committed to social justice we will emerge a force for righteousness in the world. Like passionate dreamers – no longer content with rhetoric and night-time visitations – let's imagine and surrender ourselves to dream these 'justice' dreams during the day, and to make them reality.

Campbell Roberts

In New Zealand it is honourable to say that you took part in the protest against the 1981 Rugby Tour of South Africa. But I can tell you that as I sat blocking the motorway, surrounded by helmeted police with riot shields and long batons, knowing I'd be arrested if they saw the large bolt cutters concealed up the tunic of my Salvation Army uniform, it didn't feel honourable. It felt terrifying. Sitting there on the motorway I asked myself again and again 'Why was I this stupid?'

In retrospect, social justice actions can seem like stirring stuff. But they rarely feel like it at the time. When an angry boss phones for an explanation of why you have been on the national television news (again!) supporting protesters and radicals well known for demonstrating and then getting yourself arrested at a poverty conference, the convincing explanation doesn't flow easily down the phone line.

It hurts when colleagues call you a communist because of the causes you support, and a saintly believer won't speak to you because you have been helping support the families of rubbish collectors on strike. It is not easy when a supervisor you respect deeply says in a hurt tone, 'But I trusted you and you've let me down,' because I had overlooked mentioning to him that for six weeks I lent the local church bus and mobile social service centre (with staff members), to a group of radicals walking the length of New Zealand to protest unemployment. It's scary when your arguments on television for people trigger phone calls threatening your life and family. Scary, too, when people phone the denominational leadership to say, 'This is the last time I donate to the church.' Suddenly you don't have many friends. *So why did I do it?* And why is the past thirty-five years of my Christian leadership littered with actions, controversial statements and upsets in an effort to support those at the margins of New Zealand society?

I would like to be able to say that on every occasion my efforts to bring social justice were because of my deep love and passion for God, but I doubt that it would be true. Occasionally I fear that less worthy motives of egotism and self-interest drove me – it's nice to see your name in the newspaper. I was also something of a rebel and often looking for a cause as an outlet for my rebellion. Sometimes I simply liked the people I was mixing with, and they seemed a little more interesting and human than the people down at the local church, so I didn't want to offend them by pulling out of their (often) stupid schemes. So, I confess, there were mixed motives behind some of my social engagement. But I'd still like to think that at the centre of what I have been doing in the last thirty-five years is a strong belief that, in accepting the call of God to be a Christian leader, I had to live and act with a passionate and real commitment to social justice.

Where was that passion for social justice born? Some of it certainly came from my dad, who listened daily to the BBC news and made sure that I understood who was suffering injustice and where there was need in the world. I can remember debating the struggle for self-determination in Cyprus by Archbishop Makarios, and the efforts of the rebel leader of EOKA Georgios Grivas against the occupation of Cyprus by British troops. But this learning was not just theory: I saw in my dad a man of justice. A carpenter by trade, he was often away from the house and usually it was because he was doing a building project or renovation for someone down on their luck. Dad seemed to have a natural instinct for knowing when people were suffering some injustice or need, and he was there to stand alongside them. From him I also learned the value of ecumenism at a time when it wasn't popular to mix with people from other denominations. Dad was passionately committed to community action and supporting the efforts of other Christians.

So some of my social justice passion came from my family, but it was reinforced in a big way when I entered The Salvation Army Officer Training College. One Saturday morning, while cutting the training principal's lawns as part of a work section, I became involved in an event that changed the direction of my ministry. Up until that time, my focus had been on evangelism and the thrill of preaching and teaching.

But as I cut the lawns that day, an ambulance driver asked me to help him remove a patient from a house behind the training college. The set of three houses were well known because the residents of each house (up to fifteen men stayed in each of the houses) were all alcoholics. Alcoholics who were kept in misery by a despicable landlord who had control of their welfare benefit. From this he took an exorbitant rent while giving his tenants just enough money each day to help them continue their alcohol-fuelled existence. As we entered the house we passed a number of men in various states of intoxication until, on a sodden stinking mattress, we found the patient, a formerly well-proportioned male who was now a yellowing and decaying bundle of skin and bone. As we took this very ill man out of the house, he died.

I was deeply affected by this man's death, as he seemed to be the victim of a massive injustice. His landlord's callous preoccupation with making money that left no room for concern about people's health and wellbeing had helped to kill this tenant. In the days that followed, I became clearer about what should be the emphasis of my life's work. I needed to confront evil and injustice, and ensure the lives of people were not miserable and hopeless. As I prayed it seemed that God was saying to me of the dead man 'I loved him, he was my son and they killed him.' My vocation needed to be about breaking the chains of injustice that bound other human beings.

As I left the training college and my ministry commenced, my prayer and ongoing study of scripture strengthened my conviction that I must try and do all I could to combat the injustice that left people in poverty without hope, or as victims of oppression and marginalization. In my quest for justice for others I've seen families unfairly evicted from houses, or forced to live in cars or a garage because there is no housing for them. I've seen the death of hope in a father when his son's application for a good school was rejected because he lived in the poor part of town. I've felt the terror of children escaping to a refuge from a violent father. I've been angry when I have seen how some people have been treated unjustly by government agencies, large corporations or unscrupulous individuals.

And as I've prayed about these situations, my prayers have led me to places and action that I never thought a study of holiness and the Bible would involve: on to the protest line, debating with government ministers on national television, living with a family in a derelict car on a city's main street. My prayers and biblical reflection have led to problems getting a visa to visit another country because their database labelled me as a social activist and troublemaker, and encouraged me to move an evicted family's furniture in the back door of the house while the landlord moved it out of the front.

But often at the end of such actions I've seen the reality of the joy and hope spoken of in the gospels. The hope of black South Africans as they started the journey to regain their humanity, joy in the laughter of children having their first holiday by the sea, and a mother's tears of joy as she walked through the front door of the first decent housing her family had ever lived in.

Over the years of this journey in social justice I've met and had the privilege of friendship with passionate, committed, justice-seeking individuals, some of whom have shared my faith, but many of whom didn't. God still used them and I was thankful for them. Some were victims themselves, poor, homeless, unemployed, and abused; others were politicians, government officials, clergy and fellow Christians, trade unionists, and company directors. There were anarchists and royalists, conservatives and liberals, united by a passion to bring justice in situations of injustice.

More recently, I have had the privilege of working with Christians and colleague leaders in conferences and seminars on the wider issues of injustice and the biblical call to justice. It has been a privilege to see people come alive to God and find a new dimension in their ministry as they have allowed themselves to imagine and work for a new world that is just and hopeful. It is my prayer that this may continue to happen through the challenge of this book.

I can't say I have always been or that I am always just in my own life. I still struggle to live and act justly and I often fall very short. But this has been an incredibly exciting and rewarding journey that God has taken me on, to imagine the world as God wants it to be, and to try to be part of transforming the dream into reality.

ONE: MORE THAN A DREAM

What is social justice? Once you've got beyond the trendy term, an explanation of social justice takes some time. Examining social justice is complex and means unpacking the layers of issues surrounding it. A bit like peeling an onion, a glimpse at social justice is complete only with tears and perseverance. But it is a painfully good and necessary journey.

Social justice is the idea that the world and everyone in it can live equal, safe and dignified lives. Reinforcing a social justice ideology is the belief that God created the world to live that way but the perfect world was broken by sin. In the same way that the world was broken (by choosing sin) we believe it can be made whole again (by choosing justice). Social justice is about putting our whole lives behind the sacrifice of Jesus on the cross, and partnering with Him in redeeming the whole world.

Although complex, social justice is also basic to our lives. It can even be found in the playground. Children have an innate sense of justice. Just try distributing sweets unevenly and hear the instant and loud cries of injustice, 'That's not fair!' There is a deep sense within us of what's right. And when something is not right our values cry out against 'injustice'. But a deeper look at the complexity of social justice would suggest that this struggle is fought not only against the external systems but also against internal ones. It's fought against our own greed – a selfishness that allows us to accept a situation that is unjust as long as we're the ones with more. In the playground we never cared if we had more sweets than our friends, just so long they didn't have more than us!

Social justice is connected with our own humanity, damaged inside and out by sin. An understanding of this justice is the key to correcting both our internal struggle (sin) and our external issues (injustice).

To understand what social justice is, we must start by understanding *injustice*, for justice implies an action against something unjust. But when we speak of 'injustice', what do we really mean?

Injustice is anything out of line with the perfect will of God. Injustice is sin, systems, powers, and authorities that damage the world. Injustice is greed, desire and harmful practices and beliefs that diminish people and society.

There are situations that are universally understood as unjust. When Jesus told the ancient and yet constantly relevant Good Samaritan story (Luke 10:25-37), the victim had, through no fault of his own, became weak and vulnerable. He had just suffered an injustice. But what if the victim on the road to Samaria wasn't a good guy who was in the wrong place at the wrong time, as we tend to assume? Would it change the story? Would it change how we interpret the story? Should it?

There are clear and plain injustices all around us, and there are also complicated and hazy areas of injustice as well. There are many disagreements over whether something is just or not.

> To be neutral in a situation of injustice is to have chosen sides already. It is to support the status quo.
>
> Desmond Tutu

In Western countries, the public debates on economic and public policy often raise complex issues of justice:

- Should there be a limit on the amount of asylum protection given to victims of oppression in order to protect the national social and economic status quo?
- Is it just to encourage rich people to immigrate to our country while at the same time severely limiting immigration from poor countries?
- Both the proponents of the war in Iraq and on terrorism, and those opposed to them use 'justice' to support their respective views.
- Some believe justice is achieved when criminals are given long and harsh prison sentences, while others see it served when criminals are helped to reform and given mental health and addiction services to aid this process.
- Questions also arise in balancing the rights of victims and offenders.
- It is argued by some that justice is accomplished when the rich pay higher levels of tax while others believe a flat tax system is more equitable.
- Would justice be served by a carbon market that forced the developed carbon-polluting countries to buy carbon credits from poorer countries that create less carbon pollution?

These are all debatable issues, none of them easily solved, and all requiring a careful consideration of Christian thought and theology before action.

Justice and Social Policy

Welfare reform in many developed countries has suffered huge setbacks because of an emerging concept in public opinion of the 'undeserving poor'. This is an attitude that suggests that people struggle with poverty because of their own irresponsibility, and that therefore their fate is not an injustice but something brought upon themselves by their reckless action or inaction.

Generations of people have been raised on 'welfare' or government dependency. This has created a ghetto-like existence for children raised in a system who become all too familiar with its ways. Almost inevitably, the cycle of poverty is repeated and repeated again.

Visitors to a poor neighbourhood in the developed world are often shocked by the sight of cable televisions in family homes where there is no food in the fridge (and often no fridge or cooking facilities). However, these families often lack the basic life skills of cooking, budgeting and education and so their choices take on a different complexion.

It is dangerous to make quick assumptions, for a more thorough investigation often reveals a raft of painful social conditions that help explain seemingly indefensible behaviour. If you are surrounded by abuse, addiction and insecurity, the television offers a welcome escape. The answers are not easy. Understanding and achieving justice is challenging and complex.

From far away injustice often looks like an easy fix, or a generalized issue. But if we take the time to look – to really look – we often find that injustice is a complex layering of wrongs, culminating in an individual making poor choices for lack of better ones. To look at injustice simply as an 'issue' would be to miss the bigger picture. We must see injustice not only as an issue to fight, but also recognize that people 'suffer' injustice.

Injustice is something done, or conditions set down, that causes people (real people, with God-given capacity, gifts and talents) to suffer. To know and become friends with people, to choose to see, to be up close and personal, is a first step towards understanding 'injustice' and understanding the verse 'He has showed you, O man, what is good. And what does the Lord require of you? To act justly and to love mercy and to walk humbly with your God.' (Micah 6:8.)

When we think about justice we often link it with criminal justice: the need for people to be punished when they offend against the laws of the community. But social justice is more than legal and retributive justice. It's not simply about changing the law or paying people back what they deserve. It is about actively eliminating the inequalities that exist in society, and thus it is a preventative and restorative justice – creating fairness and equality in society. It is helping to create the world God wants. As the saying goes, 'An eye for an eye makes the whole world blind.'

Social justice is what faces you in the morning. It is awakening in a house with adequate water supply, cooking facilities and sanitation. It is the ability to nourish your children and send them to school where their education not only equips them for employment but also reinforces their knowledge and understanding of their cultural inheritance. It is the prospect of genuine employment and good health: a life of choices and opportunity, free from discrimination.[5]

Mick Dodson,

'Annual Report of the Aboriginal and Torres Strait Islander', Social Justice Commissioner, 1993

In order to get to this fair society we must be committed to gaining a real understanding of injustice and then setting our lives towards creating a better world. In the gospel of Luke there is a pivotal moment where

Jesus makes clear his whole purpose. 'The Spirit of the Lord is upon me, for he has anointed me to bring Good News to the poor. He has sent me to proclaim that captives will be released, that the blind will see, that the oppressed will be set free, and that the time of the Lord's favour has come.' (Luke 4:18-19, NLT)

The cost of this statement was immediate rejection and eventual death. Everything Jesus does and says and everywhere he goes after that is a journey towards the cross. He offers the sacrifice necessary to change the power of sin in our world – thus undoing the origin of injustice itself. Social justice is a complete commitment to change the world. You can ask every world-changer about the dangers of looking deep into the onion of social justice. It is not just the tears and the smell; it's the reality of what you must do in response to what you see. Jesus came as God in the flesh. He experienced a sin-filled world and fully understands its effect in a life and in a community. 'The Word became flesh and blood, and moved into the neighbourhood.' (John 1:14, MSG)

As Martin Luther King, Jr. advocated for non-violence in the black civil rights struggle across America, he experienced rejection from the young 'free Negroes' in the north, who told him that as he was from the south he couldn't understand their situation. At around the same time as King's crusades for non-violent resistance, Malcolm X was inciting a movement based on violent revolution. Coming from the south, where oppression was explicit, King didn't understand what it was to live a technically 'free' life with little freedom. So he moved his family into a Chicago slum, an urban ghetto, in true gospel style.[6] He chose to take a good, long and close up look at injustice.

'The civil rights movement had too often been middle class oriented and had not moved to the grassroots lives of our communities. So I thought the great challenge facing the civil rights movement was to move into these areas to organize and gain identity with ghetto dwellers and young people in the ghetto. This was one of the main reasons why I felt that in moving to Chicago I would live in the very heart of the ghetto. I would not only experience what my brothers and sisters experience in living conditions, but I would be able to live with them . . .

Too soon you began to see the effects of this emotional and environmental deprivation. The children's clothes were too skimpy to protect them from the Chicago wind, and a closer look revealed the mucus in the corners of their bright eyes, and you were reminded that vitamin pills and flu shots were luxuries which they could ill afford. The "runny noses" of ghetto

> *children became a graphic symbol of medical neglect in a society which had mastered most of the diseases from which they will too soon die. There was something wrong in a society which allowed this to happen.'*[7]

A similar experience is obvious in the lives of Muhammad Yunus and Amartya Sen, two highly respected economists who are both Nobel Peace Prize winners and strong advocates for the poor. They were deeply impacted by the famines that occurred in Bengal in 1943 and Bangladesh in 1974. Both came to the conclusion that the immense loss of life was unnecessary and a symptom of unequal and flawed economic and social systems.

Sen recalls, 'The memory of the Bengal famine of 1943, in which between two and three million people had died, and which I had watched from Santiniketan, was still quite fresh in my mind. I had been struck by its thoroughly class-dependent character. (I knew of no one in my school or among my friends and relations whose family had experienced the slightest problem during the entire famine; it was not a famine that afflicted even the lower middle classes – only people much further down the economic ladder, such as landless rural labourers.) Calcutta itself, despite its immensely rich intellectual and cultural life, provided many constant reminders of the proximity of unbearable economic misery, and not even an elite college could ignore its continuous and close presence.'[8]

All three men's experiences of seeing injustice and questioning it has motivated and informed the direction of their life work. Justice for all people is the call of God. It is the hope for the world. Justice is worth living for, even dying for.

Prayer

God, we pray
Give bread to those who do not have bread
And to us who have bread give the hunger for justice.

SECTION ONE:
FOUNDATIONS OF JUSTICE

TWO: BIBLICAL JUSTICE

'Neither revolution nor reformation can ultimately change a society, rather you must tell a new powerful tale, one so persuasive that it sweeps away the old myths and becomes the preferred story, one so inclusive that it gathers all the bits of our past and our present into a coherent whole, one that even shines some light into the future so that we can take the next step forward.' – Ivan Illich

In *Say to This Mountain: Mark's story of discipleship*, Ched Myers notes that the Word of God only has transforming power as it intersects with our personal and the broader collective stories and history of our communities and nation.[9]

As we ask questions of justice, it is important that we take the time to move between the biblical, individual and communal stories so that each informs the others, and that our understanding and belief in the biblical story intersects and informs how we view justice.

A Story of Justice

In *Make Poverty Personal*, Ash Barker takes a theological look at God's call to stand with the poor and urges us to engage in the biblical story. 'As Christians we need to re-read our Bibles and study such words as "oppression". There are fourteen Hebrew words for oppression. What such a study reveals is that poverty by nature mars the image of God in people, and makes it impossible to love as God intends.'[10]

As we go deeper into the Bible we discover that it is the story of God's relationship with and faithfulness to a fallen, broken, and unjust humanity. It is therefore no surprise that a dominating concern of the biblical writers is to proclaim the justice of God and to call for just conduct from people in response.

God wants a relationship with the world.

Scripture, particularly the Old Testament, has as its main emphasis God's relationship with community rather than God's relationship with individuals. Exodus is the story of a nation rescued from oppression and injustice so that relationship to God can be restored.

Justice is essential to that relationship.

As God delivers the Israelite community

- Exodus and Deuteronomy outline the rights, responsibilities and ecclesiastical structures.
- Leviticus addresses the social and environmental aspects.
- Judges establishes a legal framework.
- Samuel and Kings summarize the characteristics and qualities required from the monarchy and national leadership.
- The prophets constantly remind the people that injustice offends God, offering graphic pictures of the injustice and desolation within the nation. The prophets record the consequences of ignoring relationship with God and the injustice that arises within community as a result. They describe the actions of justice required to restore the nation.

Through prophets such as Amos, God warns Israel that they will be judged and punished for their sins. In particular God condemns them for their treatment of the oppressed and disadvantaged and calls for justice:

> 'Listen to this message that the Lord has spoken against you, O people of Israel and Judah – against the entire family I rescued from Egypt: "From among all the families on the earth, I have been intimate with you alone. That is why I must punish you for all your sins."' (Amos 3:1-2, NLT)
>
> 'They have perverted justice by selling honest people for silver and poor people for a pair of sandals. They trample helpless people in the dust and deny justice to those who are oppressed.' (Amos 2:6, adapted from TNIV)
>
> 'You twist justice, making it a bitter pill for the oppressed. You treat the righteous like dirt.' (Amos 5:7, NLT)

Our God is relational, so it should be no surprise that biblical justice is about relationships. At the roots of biblical justice is the creation and sustaining of right relationships with God and between people. God is just because he remains faithful to his covenant with Israel. He can be relied upon to honour his commitment to Israel and calls her to faithfulness as well. This includes obeying God's stipulations to protect the poor and weak and to dispense justice equitably.

Justice, in biblical terms, means doing all that is necessary to maintain healthy, equitable and life-giving relationships between people. Biblical justice seeks to put wrong relationships right, and to reconstruct or redeem situations to create restored relationships.

A God of Justice

A constant theme among prophets like Jeremiah is linking knowing God with doing justice. The prophetic understanding was that you cannot claim to know God if you are not committed to doing justice.

> 'Thus says the Lord: "Let not the wise man boast in his wisdom, let not the mighty man boast in his might, let not the rich man boast in his riches, but let him who boasts boast in this, that he understands and knows me, that I am the Lord who practices steadfast love, justice, and righteousness in the earth. For in these things I delight, declares the Lord."' (Jeremiah 9:23-4, ESV)

> The very universe of God is on the side of justice
>
> Martin Luther King, Jr.

If we want to know and understand God, we must understand his passion for justice. This is radically different from the contemporary understanding of 'knowing God' that is typically expressed in contemporary worship.

Following God's condemnation of Israel's sin, Amos delivers a scathing message:

> 'I hate, I despise your feasts, and I take no delight in your solemn assemblies. Even though you offer me your burnt offerings and grain offerings, I will not accept them; and the peace offerings of your fattened animals, I will not look upon them.
>
> Take away from me the noise of your songs; to the melody of your harps I will not listen. But let justice roll down like waters, and righteousness like an ever-flowing stream.' (Amos 5:21-4, ESV)

Biblical justice is not an abstract concept. It is an active power, for it is acting out the nature of God. This is different from simply upholding the law or defending the status quo; it is about living out the justice we see in the nature of God. Such justice requires constant action to deliver the oppressed, restrain the oppressors, heal the broken-hearted and feed the hungry.

The enormous concern for justice in the Bible derives from the fact that justice is considered to be an attribute of God. Justice belongs to the very character of God.

> 'For all his ways are justice. A God of faithfulness and without iniquity, just and upright is he.' (Deuteronomy 32:4, ESV)

The centrality of justice to the nature of God explains how the biblical writers can therefore condemn injustice not only in Israel but also in surrounding nations. The God who creates all people holds nations accountable to establish justice for all in their laws and practice. There is a striking picture of this in Psalm 82 when Yahweh attends an international congress of gods and accuses other gods of injustice in other nations.

> 'God has taken his place in the divine council; in the midst of the gods he holds judgement:
>
> "How long will you judge unjustly and show partiality to the wicked?"
>
> Give justice to the weak and the fatherless; maintain the right of the afflicted and the destitute. Rescue the weak and the needy; deliver them from the hand of the wicked.' (Psalm 82:1-4, ESV)

So deeply understood was God's just nature that the biblical writers often express annoyance and puzzlement at the way God puts up with the injustice and lack of righteousness of his people. Habakkuk records:

> 'You who are of purer eyes than to see evil and cannot look at wrong, why do you idly look at traitors and remain silent when the wicked swallows up the man more righteous than he?' (Habakkuk 1:13, ESV)

Israel knew that God was a God of justice. They had seen that justice in action. As a nation, they had been the recipients of it. God had intervened when they were subject to injustice from the Egyptians and he had also acted to save Israel from their unjust neighbours. Justice was embedded in their law, which required people to act towards each other in ways that characterized the nature of God.

> 'You shall have just balances, just weights, a just ephah, and a just hin: I am the Lord your God, who brought you out of the land of Egypt.' (Leviticus 19:36, ESV)

For the biblical writers justice was rooted in the very character of God.

The Good News

Jesus is the proclaimer of God's justice. In keeping with the messianic expectation, Jesus represents the triumph of God's justice on the earth. His message spoke into the prevailing concern of the time, which was the injustice that surrounded God's people in everyday life. Jesus was the incarnation of their hope for justice. Matthew describes Jesus as that which was foretold and hoped for by Isaiah in Isaiah 42:

> 'Behold, my servant whom I have chosen, my beloved with whom my soul is well pleased. I will put my Spirit upon him, and he will proclaim justice to the Gentiles. He will not quarrel or cry aloud, nor will anyone hear his voice in the streets; a bruised reed he will not break, and a smouldering wick he will not quench, until he brings justice to victory; and in his name the Gentiles will hope.' (Matthew 12:18-21, ESV)

Jesus described his own ministry as bringing justice to the poor, and he cast himself in that hope

> 'The Spirit of the Lord is upon me, because he has anointed me to proclaim good news to the poor. He has sent me to proclaim liberty to the captives and recovering of sight to the blind, to set at liberty those who are oppressed.' (Luke 4:18, ESV)

Jesus calls us into this ministry with him and warns us through a parable that on judgement day, as sheep and goats, we will be separated according to how we treated 'the least of these'. Furthermore, only the righteous will have eternal life (Matthew 25:31-46). To be righteous means to act justly towards our neighbour.

If there are any remaining doubts about the call to God's people to minister justice in our present world we only need study the life, ministry, death and resurrection of Jesus.

The Partiality of Biblical Justice

The statue of Lady Justice in Washington, DC has scales signifying right and duties, a sword representing power to punish wrongdoings and a blindfold indicating impartiality. Impartiality means that everyone is treated the same, without favouritism on basis of gender, race, wealth, education or class.

Impartiality rightly lies at the heart of our criminal and civil justice system today. The same is true of the criminal and civil justice systems in the Old Testament. Judges are to show no partiality on the basis of social status.

> 'And I charged your judges at that time, "Hear the cases between your brothers, and judge righteously between a man and his brother or the alien who is with him. You shall not be partial in judgement. You shall hear the small and the great alike. You shall not be intimidated by anyone, for the judgement is God's. And the case that is too hard for you, you shall bring to me, and I will hear it." ' (Deuteronomy 1:16-17, ESV)
>
> 'You shall not pervert justice. You shall not show partiality, and you shall not accept a bribe, for a bribe blinds the eyes of the wise and subverts the cause of the righteous.' (Deuteronomy 16:19, ESV)

Impartiality is at the heart of criminal and civil justice, but when it comes to social justice a different emphasis emerges. With respect to social justice (defined here as how wealth and power is distributed in the society) scripture requires definite partiality or bias towards one section of the population.

The justice of God requires that there is special concern shown to the poor, the widows, the orphans, and the immigrants referred to in scripture as the aliens. In fact, the litmus test of scripture on whether justice is being done is the plight of the poor and the needy in society. The true measure of justice is how the most vulnerable members of the community are treated.

> 'Do not ill-treat an alien or oppress him, for you were aliens in Egypt. Do not take advantage of a widow or an orphan. If you do and they cry out to me, I will certainly hear their cry. My anger will be aroused, and I will kill you with the sword; your wives will become widows and your children fatherless.' (Exodus 22:21-24)[11]

Most people are worried by the concept of bias and consider that partiality seems contrary to the term justice. But what scripture recognizes is that treating people the same will not achieve justice when a large power imbalance exists.

The Psalms again express bias:

> 'Who made heaven and earth,
> The sea and all that is in them;
> Who keeps faith forever;
> Who executes justice for the oppressed;
> Who gives food to the hungry.
> The Lord sets the prisoners free.
> The Lord opens the eyes of the blind.
> The Lord raises up those who are bowed down;
> The Lord loves the righteous;
> The Lord protects the strangers;
> He supports the fatherless and the widow,
> But He thwarts the way of the wicked.' (Psalm 146:6-9, NASB)

God's justice is rightly biased in favour of the poor and oppressed for two main reasons.

Firstly, the poor are more frequently the victims of injustice than others. Their God-given rights are more easily trampled on than the rich and powerful.

Secondly, the way the poor are forced to live violates God's purpose for the world.

God is therefore not so much biased *towards* the poor as he is biased *against* poverty and oppression.

Grinding poverty, homelessness and hunger are evil and contrary to God's will and purpose. God's perfect world does not involve some people lacking basic needs while others live in opulence and wealth. That is why, in scripture, meeting the needs of the poor is not seen as an act of charity but an act of justice. This work moves the world in the direction of God's intention for it. Charity can enslave a population: consider welfare dependency, for example. Justice does not enslave, but liberates, because it seeks to empower the weak so that they can participate fully in society.

The Biblical Triangle: Faith, Mercy and Justice

In *The Little Book of Biblical Justice* Chris Marshall describes the relationship of faith, mercy and justice before describing the nature of that justice.

When we consider the following three passages alongside each other, several things emerge about the essence of God's will, the heart of God's law, and the meaning of God's Kingdom

> 'And what does the Lord require of you but to *do justly*, to *love mercy*, and to *walk humbly* with your God?' (Micah 6:8, NKJV)
>
> 'Woe to you, scribes and Pharisees, hypocrites! For you tithe mint and dill and cumin, and have neglected the weightier matters of the law: *justice* and *mercy* and *faithfulness*. These you ought to have done, without neglecting the others.' (Matthew 23:23, ESV)
>
> 'For the kingdom of God is not a matter of eating and drinking but of righteousness [*justice*] and *peace* and *joy* in the Holy Spirit.' (Romans 14:17, ESV)

In Matthew 23, Jesus teaches that it is fundamental to read scripture and construct theology in light of God's primary values, the things God regards as the most important: justice, mercy and faithfulness. Our relationship with God could be described as a triangle of faith, mercy (or peace) and justice. Scripture does not present them as competing aspects, or suggest that one flows out of the other; rather, they are a triangle that forms the basis of our relationship with God.

Micah 6:8 Triangle

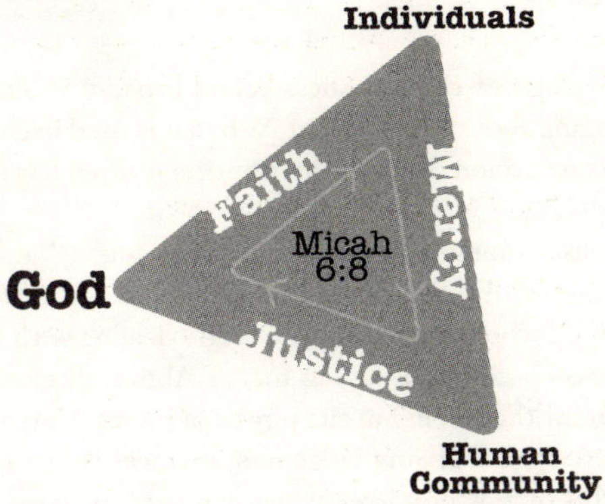

Each text places justice or righteousness first on the list. Justice is not an optional extra. *It is our first activity.* Justice is the first and primary demand that God places on his people. As a God of justice (or righteousness), he expects that we, his community, be his agents for bringing justice to bear in the world; to usher in a just society without discrimination and with fair treatment and equality for all.

In modern usage 'righteousness' often carries the understanding of personal morality, or religious piety, while justice relates to public, judicial fairness and equal rights. But in the Bible 'righteousness' often includes what we mean by 'justice'. Righteousness in the Bible conveys the idea of doing justice and it may lead us to some new understandings if we use versions of scripture that recognize this more frequently.

An interesting exercise is to take some well known biblical references and substitute the word 'justice' for 'righteousness'. Consider these verses from the Sermon on the Mount:

> 'Blessed are those who hunger and thirst for justice, for they will be filled.' (Matthew 5:6)
>
> 'Blessed are those who are persecuted because of justice, for theirs is the kingdom of heaven.' (Matthew 5:10)
>
> 'For I tell you that unless your justice surpasses that of the Pharisees and the teachers of the law, you will certainly not enter the kingdom of heaven.' (Matthew 5:20)

> 'But seek first his kingdom and his justice, and all these things will be given to you as well.' (Matthew 6:33)

'The biblical language of righteousness refers broadly to doing, being, declaring or bringing about what is right. When it is used in contexts that deal with conflict, coercion or social distribution it often has the force of justice or justice making.'[12]

Next on the list comes mercy. Scripture uses 'mercy' almost exclusively in connection with God. Most references to mercy in the Bible are descriptions of God who is rich in mercy. God's dealing with our broken humanity is characterized by a loving mercy. Above all else Christians should be known for their belief in the power of mercy. Not, as our reputation sometimes suggests, being judgemental voices in the community. But what does this mercy look like? What it meant for Jesus was acting mercifully toward those that cry out for help in our communities, such as the orphan and widow, and including those the Pharisees excluded.

In *Can You Hear Me?* Brad Jersak helps us compare mercy and justice without playing them against each other as opposites:

> *'Mercy helps those who have not received what they deserve (by the way of basic human rights) and relents from inflicting punishment on those who deserve it. Justice makes sure everyone gets what he or she deserves (by way of human rights and freedoms but also penalties for wrongs done). Grace adds to justice the additional blessings and gifts that we definitely do not deserve.*
>
> *Mercy is like the ambulance at the bottom of a cliff, ready to help those who fall. Justice builds a fence at the top of the cliff to protect them from falling in the first place (Deuteronomy 22:8).*
>
> *Mercy wipes the tears from the eyes. Justice asks, "Why are you crying?"*
>
> *Mercy welcomes the hungry to gather around God's banqueting table. Justice addresses why some are under the table aching of hunger while others are sitting on top of the table aching from gluttony. Mercy seeks and saves those lost in the darkness. Justice asks, "Why is it dark? Who is keeping it dark? Who is benefiting from the darkness? Is it I, Lord?"'*[13]

Finally, all three biblical texts mention our personal faith and experience of God last, not first. This is in direct contrast to what has perhaps become the hallmark of modern evangelicalism, with its emphasis on the individual and privatized 'God experience' rather than on mercy and justice.

Five Points about Injustice

To understand the mission field which we are called to, we must understand injustice and what God thinks about it.

God calls injustice sin
We often dismiss injustice, poverty, trafficking, homelessness and hunger as the result of poor social, economic, or political policy. It is vital for us to understand that injustice grieves God and is contrary to his will and purpose.

Injustice has a devastating impact on individuals, families, communities and nations.

Seeing injustice as sin moves us to view the world through biblical theology and engages our discipleship in a new way. This is not simply social service or social action; it is the wider work of redemption. When we start seeing the world as God sees it this decreases the possibility that we may simply change the world to suit ourselves. *Biblical justice is about seeing the world through the eyes of God.*

Often the Christian community is divided into two camps: those who emphasize personal salvation from sin over social reform and those who emphasize social reform over personal sin. We suggest they are intimately connected. Ultimately, when you boil social justice down to its most basic form, it is about right relationships. Sin results in broken relationships, between one another and between humanity and God. The only true social transformation happens from the inside out. It is the transforming presence of the Kingdom of God in the world that ensures the true presence of justice. This happens at both a personal and community level. Social justice is not in one camp, it is the essence of both.

Injustice breaks the heart of God
The suffering and the oppressed are God's children. God is affected by sin and injustice. God expects that we, his disciples, will be moved to do something about it. We are all God's children, so when injustice occurs, it is in the family. Christianity connects its followers to the suffering of our sisters and brothers in this uniquely powerful way. What we do to the powerless of the world we do to God. We are then asked to challenge injustice.

How does God feel when little children are trafficked as sex objects?

Injustice is contagious

It spreads like a cancer throughout the world. Martin Luther King, Jr. once said, 'Injustice anywhere is a threat to justice everywhere.' When we allow injustice to go unchecked it's like cancer, it gets worse naturally. Just because we don't experience some injustice personally does not mean we are not connected to or affected by that evil. What starts small grows and repeats.

A child caught in sexual exploitation without intervention often becomes an exploiter. On and on goes the ever-increasing cycle of injustice. Generations of families who have suffered an injustice continue to breed the results of that injustice. Many children of war veterans who had experienced psychological trauma suffered emotional outbursts and disassociation from their parents, and now struggle to parent with proper emotional connection. Where does the cycle end?

'The only thing necessary for evil to triumph is for good people to do nothing.'

Edmund Burke

Challenging injustice can bring persecution

Often there is a cost associated with challenging injustice. Sometimes we will be applauded for our action and at other times criticized and suffer for it.

Archbishop Oscar Romero understood this principle well as he engaged in a social justice campaign in Columbia. While performing a funeral mass in the Chapel of Divine Providence Hospital, he was shot dead by a paid assassin.

Only moments before his death, Romero had reminded the mourners of the parable of wheat. His prophetic words were:

> *'Those who surrender to the service of the poor through love of Christ will live like the grain of wheat that dies . . . The harvest comes because of the grain that dies . . . We know that every effort to improve society,*

> *above all when society is so full of injustice and sin, is an effort that God blesses; that God wants; that God demands of us.'*[14]

Jesus put it like this, 'God blesses you when people mock you and persecute you and lie about you and say all sorts of evil things against you because you are my followers.' (Matthew 5:11, NLT)

Facing injustice poses challenging questions

We like resolutions, and particularly happy endings. The challenge for us is to live with the tension. In *God's Politics* Jim Wallis says that one of the principles of his life is 'to never stop asking hard questions'. Asking questions is how we uncover injustice.

Some of those challenging questions are:

- What is the extent and nature of injustice and suffering in our world?
- What are the real causes of injustice and suffering?
- What social or political factors might keep these problems in place?
- What needs to happen to remove these global scourges of injustice and suffering?

How Are We Personally Linked to Injustice?

If God calls injustice sin, we are implicated. Sins of commission are often thought of as 'action sins', or things we have done against someone or God. Sins of omission are things we haven't done. Both are our responsibility.

Injustice today is often a combination of *commission* (done in secret, such as corporate executives exploiting developing world labourers) and *omission* (fuelled by our own personal greed, such as when we buy the cheapest clothes on the market and don't ask who made them and under what conditions). These are the personal implications of injustice as sin. We are implicit in the relationship.

Some Questions to Ask the Lord

Would you please take me deep enough into your heart to sense your concern for justice, mercy and faith?

As I tune in to those themes, is there some grief in your heart about an area or people group or issue that you would like to share with me? Let me see it how you see it. Let me feel how you feel.

What is the darkness that is prevailing there? Why is it there? What needs to happen there? What promise do you have for them?

What do you want me to pray? What do you want me to say? What do you want me to do? If you need a spokesperson, I am available. To whom should I go? How shall I deliver this message? What is the word of hope? What will redemption look like?

If this were your first time doing such an exercise, I would suggest writing out your message and then pray (and perhaps fast) over it until peace comes. Then ask the Lord what action you can take with a pure heart.[15]

Prayer

May God bless us with discomfort at easy answers,
half-truths and superficial relationships,
so that we may live deeply in your heart.
May God bless us with anger at injustice,
oppression and exploitation of people
so that we may work for justice, freedom and peace.
May God bless us with tears to shed for those who suffer from pain,
rejection, starvation and war so that we may reach out our hand to
comfort them and turn their pain to joy.
And may God bless us with enough foolishness to believe we can make
a difference in the world.
(Franciscan Benediction)

JESUS' NEW ECONOMY OF GRACE

Ched Myers

Jesus and Jubilee . . .

Discipleship thus means forsaking the seductions and false securities of the debt system for a re-communitized economy of enough for everyone. In such an economy, which Jesus calls the 'kingdom', there are no longer any rich and poor – by definition, therefore, the rich 'cannot enter' it (Mark 10:23-25). So contrary is this vision to our accepted horizons of possibility, however, that disciples ancient and modern have difficulty truly believing (Mark 10:26).

Jesus' call for radical social restructuring at all levels, from the household (Mark 3:31-35) to the body politic (Mark 10:35-45), is summarized by the Jubilee ultimatum: 'Many who are first will be last, and the last first' (Mark 10:31). He typically chooses the venue of table fellowship in order to both show and tell object lessons that illustrate this. Meals lay at the heart of ancient society: where, what, and with whom you ate defined your social identity and status. Thus the table was a 'mirror' of society, with its economic classes and political divisions.

In the extended banquet story in Luke 14, Jesus systematically undermines prevailing conventions and proprieties, while advocating a new 'table' of compassion and equality. The opening episode deals (not surprisingly) with a dispute over the Sabbath practice (Luke 14:1-6). Next comes Jesus' attack on the dominant system of meritocracy, with its hierarchies, prestige posturing, and ladder climbing, and his invitation to 'downward mobility' (verses 7-11). He then offends his host by criticizing his guest list, rejecting the reciprocal patronage system of the elite, and calling instead for a focus upon 'those who cannot repay' (verses 12-14). The series concludes with Jesus' pointed little fable about an exemplary host who finally understands the bankruptcy of meritocracy and decides instead to build a Jubilee community with the poor and outcast (verses 15-24).

Grace versus Mammon

There is no theme more common to Jesus' storytelling than Sabbath economics. He promises poor sharecroppers abundance (Mark 4:3-8, 26-32), but threatens absentee landowners (Mark 12:1-12) and rich householders

(Luke 16:19-31) with judgment. In order to teach the incompatibility of the economy of grace with the dictates of 'Mammon', Jesus spins a parable that portrays a hapless middleman caught in the brutal logic of the debt system who decides to 'trade' instead in Jubilee-style debt release (Luke 16:1-13). When faced with a dispute over inheritance rights, Jesus counters with a parable about the folly of storing up wealth (remember the manna!), and then exhorts us to learn the lessons of grace and subsistence from the 'great economy' of nature (Luke 12:13-34; see James 5:1-6).

These are some of the 'Jubilee footprints' in the Jesus story. It is important to note that the early church which produced these gospels also *practiced* Sabbath economics. The most obvious example – similarly maligned or ignored by modern exegetes – is the Acts account of the coming of the Spirit at Pentecost – the Jubilee-tinged celebration of *Shavuot* (Acts 2). This occasions a portrait of the church's first experiment in wealth redistribution, echoing the manna story with the report that 'assets were distributed to any as had need' (Acts 2:45, 4:35). Similarly, central to the itinerant ministry of the apostle Paul was his invitation to the new Gentile churches to learn Sabbath economics by practicing interchurch mutual aid. Significantly, in his most elaborate articulation of this commitment (2 Corinthians 8-9), the *one* scriptural justification Paul employs is a citation of the manna story: 'As it is written, "those who had much did not have too much; and those who had little did not have too little" ' (2 Corinthians 8:14-15)!

Ched Myers was a writer, teacher, and activist based in Los Angeles, and a Sojourners *contributing editor, when this article appeared.*[16]

THREE: CHRISTIAN FOUNDATIONS

Following the tradition of Jesus, the history of the church is a model of social justice progression. The emerging group of believers dealt with slavery, economic oppression, gender bias and even political issues with an amazing vigour of faith that was alive in everyday issues of their time. The examples are virtually endless. Even in more recent history the Christian church is littered with stellar examples of social reformers who, through their understanding of scripture, changed the world. It would be exciting to look at many more examples around the globe, but here are a life example and a case study from the UK to whet your appetite for social change.

1. Elizabeth Fry – Elizabeth Fry Society
2. William Booth – The Salvation Army

Elizabeth Fry

Elizabeth Fry was a Quaker who became famous for her work to reform the prison system in Britain in the early nineteenth century. Not only a great social reformer, Elizabeth Fry also defied the restrictions of her day by playing a fuller role in society. It was fortunate for all concerned that Quakers believed in the equality of women (250 years before they won the vote), otherwise Elizabeth Fry's unusual talents in the area of prison reform might never have been realized. Her actions served to change the world and the culture as other women became inspired to get involved in social reform.

In 1812 she wrote in her diary *'I fear that my life is slipping away to little purpose'*. Not long afterwards, a man called Stephen Grellet came to see her to ask for help. He was a French aristocrat who had gone into exile because of the French Revolution. In America he had become a Quaker. While visiting Britain he had been given permission to visit some prisons, and had been horrified by the conditions he had seen in the women's prison in Newgate. He found prisoners lying on the bare stone floors, and some newborn babies without clothing. He went to Elizabeth Fry, who immediately sent out for warm material and asked other women Friends to help her make clothes for the babies. Elizabeth Fry took the invitation to see injustice and then match it with the presence of hope, life and light.

The next day she went with her sister-in-law to Newgate prison. At first the turnkeys did not want to let her in as the women prisoners were wild and savage, but physical danger did not frighten her in the way that public speaking and audiences did. Elizabeth and her sister-in-law did go in, and were very shocked at the conditions they found there – particularly when they saw two women stripping the clothes from a dead baby to give them to another child. They gave out the warm clothes for the babies and comforted the ill prisoners. Next day they returned with more warm clothes and with clean straw for the sick to lie on. On a third visit she prayed for the prisoners, who were moved by her sincere words of love for them.

After visiting London's notorious Newgate prison in 1813, the banker's daughter became not just the UK's most important woman penal reformer, but Europe's chief campaigner for inmates' rights.

'Punishment is not for revenge, but to lessen crime and reform the criminal,' declared Fry, at a time when prisons were more overcrowded dungeons than redemptive institutions.

The small beginnings of a woman who was obedient to her faith and who took the opportunity in front of her became the presence of justice in the world. Although most of her life was spent in England, she did visit Ireland and continental Europe. She also offered advice to the Americas, Russia and Australia. She was a strong proponent of humane treatment for prisoners and regarded by many as a leading expert in prison reform. She died in 1845 at the age of sixty-six. The Elizabeth Fry Society still has multiple units around the world, continuing to advocate for prison reform and the rights of women.[17]

William Booth

William Booth, founder of the Salvation Army, is undoubtedly one of UK's greatest Christian social reformers.

In the 1860s, the industrial revolution had transformed the cities of Britain in a dramatic way. Half the population of England now inhabited the crowded, infested, chaotic English cities. For all the advantages brought about by the Industrial Revolution, it also produced a kind of rampant individualism. Many people were inspired by thoughts of getting rich, and often this manifested itself in a self-centred attitude and a relentless drive to make money. The strong embraced such individualism. The weak were often devastated and abused by it. There was a lack of social planning and various groups emerged as social and economic forces that determined the overall direction of society. Those who were given charity were characterized as 'deserving', and usually defined as those who didn't threaten the established order.

The urban masses lived in extreme poverty and worked long hours in unsafe conditions. Vices both great and small became part of the everyday life of these people. At the time, a debate raged about why this state of chaos existed.

Some argued:

- It was caused by drink and riotous living.
- The people have lazy and indolent attitudes.
- They're not willing to work or take the opportunities available.

Those benefiting most by the industrial reform process were often the perpetuators of such arguments.

Another view came from the churches, humanitarian organizations and social reformers who identified problems such as:

- Poor social planning.
- Individualism without care or regard for others.
- Loss of jobs and a lack of upskilling.
- Unemployment.
- Inadequate housing.
- Poor wages (meaning someone could work long hours and still be unable to provide the basics of life).
- Unsafe working conditions.
- Lack of health services.
- Discrimination against and lack of emancipation for women.

William Booth grappled with these two points of view. His new Christian movement needed a firm theological underpinning for its work. Was it the personal sin of these people that led to laziness, a lack of individual effort and the failure to take responsibility for themselves? If so, the ministry emphasis needed to be on the individual sin of the person. Or were these people the victims of a selfishly individualistic society that had failed to properly organize itself so that adequate opportunities existed for all?

The reform process had moved so quickly that appropriate structures of social safety were not in place. If this were true, these people were sinned against and the ministry focus should be on the addressing of corporate evils and sin – an approach which inevitably involved politics.

Booth resolved to hold firmly to the concept of individual responsibility and personal sin but identified what he termed a 'submerged tenth' who were the sinned against. He commenced the famous *In Darkest England* reform scheme: a programme of social and political reform and action.

This scheme was built around what Booth called the 'Cab Horse Charter'. Booth found it both a stigma and an enigma that in a nineteenth-century civilized society 'our horses are better treated than our fellow human beings.' He said, 'When a horse is down he is helped up, and while he lives he has food, shelter and work. That, although a humble standard, is at present unattainable by some of our fellow men and women in this country.' [18]

Booth seems to have identified that his young Salvation Army needed to be about justice if it was to do the work of God properly.

Recent History

In the more recent history of The Salvation Army, there has been less emphasis on justice in both theology and missiology. They, like the larger Christian church, have been captured by a theology of the 'God experience'. A question present-day Christians need to grapple with is whether this emphasis on the 'God experience' has meant that in the areas of ecclesiology, theology and missiology we have failed to give significant recognition to the essential nature of a ministry of justice, especially as this is something the Bible requires for an interactive relationship with God?

We rejoice in the church's strong emphasis on faith that has brought thousands into an experience of God. We are also glad that internationally we have responded with mercy to people suffering desperate homelessness, hunger and want. In times of global catastrophe – tsunami, conflict, earthquake or storm – we have shown that we understand mercy.

But have we understood and been a people of justice? Often the church has recognized the greatest commandments of Christ as a dual mission – faith and mercy – like a bird with two wings. But understanding our relationship with God as having only two primary implications is, we contend, the essence of our problem; because we fail to integrate an understanding of justice into what it means to be in relationship with God.

The Tension of Justice

The balancing of faith, mercy and justice is not a new tension; it was also obvious in the ministry of William Booth. Booth's early work as a pawnbroker's assistant brought him into contact with the harshness and deprivation of poverty. He saw for himself its impact and destructiveness on human life. As recent biographers suggest, the impact of poverty continued to influence Booth for his entire ministry.[19] But despite this, Booth struggled with the theology of it all. Although encouraging his soldiers to relieve social need and engage in social justice actions such as the Purity Crusade of 1885, he seems to have held reservations.

On the 10th November, 1885 he wrote[20]

> *'I am sure our work has materially suffered by our attention being taken from it to give to the Purity Crusade; we may have been paid back to a certain extent, and in the long run much good may be done, but I thoroughly believe in "Salvation" being the panacea for the world's sin and sorrow, and that while there are other medicines that look in the same direction the largest amount of good can be accomplished, with the least expenditure of time and money, by simply getting the people's souls saved and keeping them saved.'*

In his recent biography of Booth, Roger J. Green recognizes that his theology developed past this rather narrow concept of redemption. 'By 1890 Booth was convinced that it was theologically correct to address social redemption systematically.'[21] He then quotes Booth 'Why all this apparatus of temples and meeting houses to save men from perdition in a world which is to come, while never . . . stretching out to save them from the inferno of their present life.' [22]

Booth's writing and speaking in the *In Darkest England and the Way Out* campaign, which for a period completely absorbed his international campaigns, is testimony to this developed theology.

> *'The scheme of social salvation is not worth discussing which is not as wide as the scheme of eternal salvation set forth in the gospel. The glad tidings must be to every creature not merely to an elect few who are to be saved . . . It is now time to fling down the false idol, and proclaim a temporal salvation as full, free and universal, and with no other limitations than the whosoever of the gospel.'* [23]

However, despite these moments of certainty when biblical justice was fully embraced and proclaimed, Booth's tension still remained – as evidenced in a letter to his son, Bramwell Booth:

> *'I cannot go in for any more "campaigns" against evils. My hands and heart are full enough. And moreover these reformers of society have no sympathy with The Salvation Army nor with Salvation from worldliness and sin. Our campaign is againt sin!'* [24]

Booth seems to have had difficulty in consistently integrating the three aspects of the biblical triangle of faith, mercy and justice. Viewing the totality of his ministry, they were all present, but at particular times he found difficulty in giving *balance* to these three aspects of biblical truth. Also, Booth tended to see mercy and justice flowing from personal faith and this led him to be suspicious of social reformers like W.T. Stead, and Frank Smith,[25] who wanted to redeem the present world.

Theological Ambivalence

This theological ambivalence towards the biblical call for justice has continued to plague the church through to the present day. Our theological pragmatism and involvement with people has ensured a consistent and outstanding ministry of spontaneous and organized mercy to the needy of the world, but in areas of justice the church has been less surefooted. Where we have become involved it has tended to be around areas of personal morality rather than structural evil. The reasons we have been weak in giving expression to the biblical theme of justice are diverse and at times difficult to discern.

Inadequate theological and biblical reflection has led to a tension between personal salvation and the need to redeem present social evil. Where we do give expression to redeeming social evil it is usually with emphasis on ministries of charity rather than justice.

In our consideration of spirituality and holiness teaching, we have been stronger in a holiness approach with its heavy emphasis on personal experience and application of holy living rather than the wider and, we think, richer approach with community emphasis. Interestingly, the first mention of holiness in the scriptures, which comes in Exodus, is connected to the call/invitation of God to be a kingdom of priests and a holy nation – at the heart of holiness is the communal practice of 'everything that is God'.

Stories of Social Justice

In their book *Insane: The Stories of Crazy Salvos Who Changed the World*, Nealson Munn and David Collinson tell the story of the 'Lights in Darkest England' enterprise in which 'The Salvation Army launched a war on sweated labour and phossy jaw'.

> *'A War Cry advertisement of July 1891 announced:*
>
> *Lights in Darkest England – The Salvation Army Social Matches! Are now ready and orders can be executed forthwith. Everybody should use the "Darkest England Safeties," which are manufactured under healthy conditions and are entirely free from the phosphorous which causes "Matchmaker's Leprosy" . . .'*[26]

The lifespan of the commercial venture was limited but the success of the 'war' was seen in 1892 when the government changed legislation around ventilation ordinances to decrease the rate of 'phossy jaw': an agonizing and disfiguring disease caused by exposure to the white phosphorous used in manufacturing matches. That was just the beginning of a series of changes in legislation that eventually outlawed the production of phosphorus matches in 1910.

Another legendary story is that of 'The Maiden Tribute of Modern Babylon'. Having been exposed to the injustice of the underground world of prostitution, Bramwell Booth and William Thomas Stead hatched a plan 'to expose the full horror of child prostitution by buying a girl and shipping her to the Continent, proving beyond doubt how easy it was to accomplish such a thing, and, by implication, how regularly it was in fact done. The story would then be publicized in Stead's magazine, the *Pall Mall Gazette*.'[27]

So successful was the campaign and the furore created by the articles that it saw the House of Commons raise the age of consent to sixteen.[28]

Hunger for Justice

Today, there is a growing hunger within the universal church for social justice. This hunger represents an opportunity to explore the relationship of faith, mercy and justice in the church. It's a hunger for justice, and according to Jesus we are blessed for 'those who hunger and thirst for righteousness [justice] . . . will be filled.' (Matthew 5:6)

The examples of Elizabeth Fry and William Booth, and other social reformers of the past who rose to the challenge of ushering in God's Kingdom on earth, should inspire and inform us to continue the expansion of the reign of Christ. May His Kingdom come.

Prayer: Praise for the Past and Trust for the Future

Living God,
We come to worship you,
Praising you for the past
And trusting you for the future!
We come to join our will to your will,
To make your purpose our purpose,
And your love our love.
We come in the name of Jesus Christ our Lord.
Amen.

THE CAB HORSE CHARTER

William Booth

What then is the standard towards which we may venture to aim with some prospect of realization in our time? It is a very humble one, but if realized it would solve the worst problems of modern Society. It is the standard of the London Cab Horse. When in the streets of London a Cab Horse, weary or careless or stupid, trips and falls and lies stretched out in the midst of the traffic there is no question of debating how he came to stumble before we try to get him on his legs again. The Cab Horse is a very real illustration of poor broken-down humanity; he usually falls down because of overwork and underfeeding.

If you put him on his feet without altering his conditions, it would only be to give him another dose of agony; but first of all you'll have to pick him up again. It may have been through overwork or underfeeding, or it may have been all his own fault that he has broken his knees and smashed the shafts, but that does not matter. If not for his own sake, then merely in order to prevent an obstruction of the traffic, all attention is concentrated upon the question of how we are to get him on his legs again. The load is taken off, the harness is unbuckled, or, if need be, cut, and everything is done to help him up. Then he is put in the shafts again and once more restored to his regular round of work. That is the first point. The second is that every Cab Horse in London has three things: a shelter for the night, food for its stomach, and work allotted to it by which it can earn its corn.

These are the two points of the Cab Horse's Charter. When he is down he is helped up, and while he lives he has food, shelter and work. That, although a humble standard, is at present absolutely unattainable by millions – literally by millions – of our fellow-men and women in this country. Can the Cab Horse Charter be gained for human beings? I answer, yes. The Cab Horse standard can be attained on the Cab Horse terms.[29]

SECTION TWO:
ACTING JUSTLY

The Global Village

61 Asians, 12 Europeans, 8 North Americans, 5 South Americans, 13 Africans, 1 from Oceania

50 women, 50 men

47 live in an urban area

9 disabled

33 Christian, 18 Muslims, 14 Hindus, 16 non-religious, 6 Buddhists, 13 practice other religions

43 live without basic sanitation

18 live without an improved water source

6 people own 59% of the entire wealth of the community

13 hungry or malnourished

14 can't read

Only 7 are educated at secondary level

Only 12 have a computer

Only 3 have an Internet connection

1 adult aged 15–49 has HIV/AIDS

The village spends more than US$1.12 trillion on military expenses

And only US$100 billion on development and aid

If you keep your food in a refrigerator, your clothes in your closet, have a bed to sleep in and a roof over your head, you are richer than 75% of the world's population

If you have a bank account, you are one of the 30 wealthiest people in the world

18 struggle to live on US$1 per day or less

53 struggle to live on US$2 per day or less

FOUR: GLOBAL COMMUNITY

The Emerging Global Network

Who is my neighbour?
It's no longer difficult to think of the world in terms of a global village. It's familiar. We hear about the world all the time – world news, world banks, world systems, world leaders, and of course the World Wide Web. We are more connected than we have ever been before to the global scene. But we are not only linked through the Internet, trade and our economies: we are connected through our relationships with other parts of the world. It is how we act in these relationships that determine whether we see people truly as our global village neighbours.

Sometimes our first introduction to social justice comes through mission experiences. They can help us make an essential connection with 'the world'. We come to understand that the world doesn't just consist of our suburb, our country, language and people who look and act the same. It expands our sphere to include 'others'. The more we see of the world, the more we realize that it's bigger than us. In recent times, mission trips have come to be thought of as less than useful. But although we recognize that their impact is limited in long-term programme benefits, the effect on participants through building relationships is powerful, and can translate into lives of social justice.

There is a great YouTube[30] video and website called *The Miniature Earth* which represents the world as a village of 100 people. With all existing human ratios remaining the same, the demographics would look something like this:

Jesus broke down the essentials of social justice with the story about the Good Samaritan. In the historical context of Jesus telling the story, the Jews despised Samaritans, yet it was a Samaritan man that showed compassion to the person in need. Jesus teaches us about compassion toward neighbours different from ourselves. In *Who Is My Neighbour?* Pope Benedict XVI reminded the Catholic Church that 'sharing the Eucharist gives rise to a service of charity towards neighbour, which "consists in the very fact that, in God and with God, I love even the person whom I do not like or even know". We are called to be open to all, for we are brothers and sisters, citizens of the world. We are called to see the possibility that any person anywhere can be our neighbour; we need only act as neighbour to them.'[31]

Social justice demands both global and local reaction. On one hand, we need the political will and government policies to shift the massive imbalance of power in the global community, and, on the other, we have Mother Teresa insisting that the world can be completely changed by one act of love, consistently given. When a BBC reporter was interviewing Mother Teresa, he revealed his cynicism at her small acts of mercy. He said, 'You don't believe that you can solve world hunger?' and Mother Teresa characteristically replied, 'Yes, I do'. The reporter was intrigued: 'How can you do that?' Mother Teresa often responded to such a challenge with 'One person at a time'.

> *'I never look at the masses as my responsibility. I look at the individual. I can love only one person at a time. I can feed only one person at a time. Just one, one, one. You get closer to Christ by coming closer to each other. As Jesus said, "Whatever you do to the least of my brethren, you do to me." So you begin . . . I begin. I picked up one person – maybe if I didn't pick up that one person I wouldn't have picked up 42,000. The whole work is only a drop in the ocean. But if I didn't put the drop in, the ocean would be one drop less. Same thing for you, same thing for your family, same thing in the church where you go, just begin . . . one, one, one.'*[32]

Nelson Mandela (former President of the 'new' South Africa), emerging from a miraculous circumstance in which small acts of defiance added up to a bloodless revolution, saw that globalization and the growing hunger for social justice on a world scale was creating an anthem for a generation.

> But in this new century, millions of people in the world's poorest countries remain imprisoned, enslaved, and in chains. They are trapped in the prison of poverty. It is time to set them free. Like slavery and apartheid, poverty is not natural. It is man-made and it can be overcome and eradicated by the actions of human beings.
>
> Nelson Mandela

Addressing the crowd in Trafalgar Square for the Make Poverty History event in 2005 he said, 'Sometimes it falls upon a generation to be great. You can be that great generation. Let your greatness blossom.'[33]

The Make Poverty History Campaign was founded on the belief that the world system, particularly trade rules, debt and international aid, must change in order to make poverty history. Mandela was calling for people to start caring enough, and speaking loudly enough, that political leaders will have to hear and act. Mandela was calling this generation to take up the challenge of massive social change in the global village through the power of our collective voice.

Bono, also a key advocate for the Make Poverty History and ONE Campaign asks, 'Why should I care about someone dying in Africa?' The answer is we care because that someone in Africa is our brother, our children, our mother, our father . . . we are connected.' This, in essence, is the gospel. God decided to change the entire world and did it by announcing the birth of a baby. These campaigns are all expecting incredibly big changes. These changes will come about through small acts of humanity leading to massive social change.

> *'So, we're launching the ONE campaign to unite America in the fight against AIDS and extreme poverty. We know that if we work together, we can win the fight and together we must because African people – guess what? – are equals in the eyes of God. They are our brothers and sisters; our lives are interconnected and interdependent. And this is not just some warm, fuzz feeling kind of way – they actually are equal in the eyes of God and let's start treating people, therefore, equally.' – Bono*

There is now a growing hunger to make a difference in the world. The rise of campaigns such as Make Poverty History, Stop The Traffik, and Fairtrade are evidence of it. Tiring of pleasure, people can see the lack of fulfilment and essential emptiness that is all consumerism can ultimately offer. We believe this generation is more willing to disregard the empty promise of prosperity for a better future together.

A new hope is emerging, a hope that the very hands that made poverty are the same hands that can end it. Mother Teresa spoke about this often: the refusal to blame poverty on God but rather on our own unwillingness to share. For 'God made the world rich enough to feed and clothe all human beings.'

Globalization

The results of globalization have been amazing on one level: world travel, economies connecting, mobility and technology uniting the most unlikely of people. Two childhood friends who hadn't seen each other in over a dozen years were recently reconnected through Facebook. It turned out they lived only a few blocks away from each other but were connected via a friend living on the other side of the world. That's the shrinking world we live in.

Martin Luther King, Jr. once said 'Before you've finished your breakfast this morning, you'll have relied on half the world.'[34] And that is just as true today. Tomorrow morning, we challenge you to look at the labels on your toiletries as you have a shower, on the labels of your clothes and finally the labels on the food you eat. How many countries and their workers have you already relied upon? The sugar could have come from one country, the wheat from another, and finally, where was it packaged? Processed? Transported through . . . ?

Supporters of globalization and free trade such as Jeffrey Sachs are quick to highlight the positive effects that it has had on developing countries. From 1981 to 2001, according to World Bank figures, the number of people living on $1 a day or less declined from 1.5 billion to 1.1 billion in absolute terms. In percentage terms, the number of people in developing nations living on less than a dollar a day declined from 40 per cent to 20 per cent of the population, with the greatest improvements occurring in economies rapidly reducing barriers to trade and investment.[35]

> One of the ironies of the recent success of India and China is the fear that . . . success in these two countries comes at the expense of the United States. These fears are fundamentally wrong and, even worse, dangerous. They are wrong because the world is not a zero-sum struggle . . . but rather is a positive-sum opportunity in which improving technologies and skills can raise living standards around the world.
>
> Jeffrey D. Sachs, The End of Poverty, 2005 →

In his book *The End of Poverty,* Sachs advocates for the end of extreme poverty and spends time answering why countries in Asia (as an example) have been able to take a strong foothold in the globalization process and achieve huge improvements in rates of absolute poverty whereas Africa has remained stagnant. For example, in East Asia between 1981 and 2002, the percentage of people living on less than two dollars a day decreased by 52 per cent compared to a 2.2 per cent increase in Sub-Saharan Africa.

That stark contrast shows us that globalization isn't a guaranteed outcome. It is a process that is evolving, and we need to question why it is not benefiting everyone. In his Nobel Peace Prize acceptance speech, Muhammad Yunus highlighted the dangers of globalization:

> *'I support globalization and believe it can bring more benefits to the poor than its alternative. But it must be the right kind of globalization. To me, globalization is like a hundred-lane highway criss-crossing the world. If it is a free-for-all highway, its lanes will be taken over by the giant trucks from powerful economies. Bangladeshi rickshaw will be thrown off the highway. In order to have a win-win globalization we must have traffic rules, traffic police, and traffic authority for this global highway. Rule of "strongest takes it all" must be replaced by rules that ensure that the poorest have a place and piece of the action, without being elbowed out by the strong. Globalization must not become financial imperialism.'*[36]

Watching grandparents walk with their grandchildren is a great lesson in social justice. Inevitably, the grandparents voluntarily slow down so that they can walk side by side with the children. No one has to tell them to do it; it's a natural expression of love in a relationship. Will we, the older members in the developing relationship, support creating 'traffic rules' if it means we are also slowed down occasionally? Currently, those of us in the position of privilege and power in the global village can continue increasing our standard of living (or a rich owner's profits) at the expense of the poor with little, if any retribution. Corporations seeking competitive advantage will not compromise their profit margins while others are benefiting from these unjust practices. In other words, those who are younger in the developing system can't keep up the pace.

The Fairtrade movement[37] is standing up to such exploitations and showing the market that consumers care about the rules of the game. Supporting the Fairtrade movement increases the volume on the prophetic call that farmers deserve just payment for the coffee beans they grow, and that workers be paid enough to be able to feed their families.

Those who have seen the 2006 film *Blood Diamond* will be aware of the injustice behind the diamond industry. Rapidly increasing in popularity, a conflict-free diamond is a diamond whose profits aren't used to fund wars and which is produced and mined under ethical conditions. Only diamonds that are certified and can be traced from the mine to the consumer are conflict-free diamonds. Conflict diamonds are still being sold today into the international diamond market as clean diamonds. It matters that there are human rights abuses behind the diamonds we purchase to say 'I love you.'

At the top of the globalization celebration is an aerial view of economic and personal suffering. *Who is my Neighbour?* suggests 'we are called to think and act globally in cooperation with those who benefit from globalization and in *solidarity* with those who are marginalized by it.'[38] This link is important to recognize. The Christian church has been called to stand with the marginalized. We also have a responsibility to show those in positions of power the effect that the system has on the poor.

'The response of our industrial machine is to expand its markets by creating new wants and new appetites amongst the people who can afford them. We are capable of meeting the basic needs of all the world's people but are in fact fostering further growth in the demand to the wealthy minority for goods and services far beyond what we need or is good for us.'[39]

It is important for those driving development to recognize that excessive capitalism is a problem in itself. The benefits we are experiencing from globalization have increased our standards of living and, at the same time, are threatening it. We in the West are living a lifestyle that the world cannot sustain. And it is the poorest nations which will suffer the most from the impact of climate change.

Millennium Development Goals [40]

At the Millennium Summit in September 2000 the largest gathering of world leaders in history adopted the UN Millennium Declaration, committing their nations to a new global partnership to reduce extreme poverty and setting out a series of time-bound targets, with a deadline of 2015, which have become known as the Millennium Development Goals.

The Millennium Development Goals (MDGs) are the world's time-bound and quantified targets for addressing extreme poverty in its many dimensions – income poverty, hunger, disease, lack of adequate shelter, and exclusion – while promoting gender equality, education, and environmental sustainability. They are also basic human rights – the rights of each person on the planet to health, education, shelter, and security.

Goal 1: Eradicate Extreme Hunger and Poverty

Goal 2: Achieve Universal Primary Education

Goal 3: Promote Gender Equality and Empower Women

Goal 4: Reduce Child Mortality

Goal 5: Improve Maternal Health

Goal 6: Combat HIV/AIDS, Malaria and Other Diseases

Goal 7: Ensure Environmental Stability

Goal 8: Develop a Global Partnership for Development

The world has made significant progress in achieving many of the Goals. Between 1990 and 2002 average overall incomes increased by approximately 21 percent. The number of people in extreme poverty declined by an estimated 130 million. Child mortality rates fell from 103 deaths per 1,000 live births a year to 88. Life expectancy rose from 63 years to nearly 65 years. An additional 8 percent of the developing world's people received access to water. And an additional 15 percent acquired access to improved sanitation services.

But progress has been far from uniform across the world – or across the Goals. There are huge disparities across and within countries. Within countries, poverty is greatest for rural areas, though urban poverty is also extensive, growing, and underreported by traditional indicators.

Sub-Saharan Africa is the epicentre of crisis, with continuing food insecurity, a rise of extreme poverty, stunningly high child and maternal mortality, and large numbers of people living in slums, and a widespread shortfall for most of the MDGs. Asia is the region with the fastest progress, but even there hundreds of millions of people remain in extreme poverty, and even fast-growing countries fail to achieve some of the non-income Goals. Other regions have mixed records, notably Latin America, the transition economies, and the Middle East and North Africa, often with slow or no progress on some of the Goals and persistent inequalities undermining progress on others.

In 2006, the World Bank predicted that the annual cost of developing countries to adapt to climate change could be anywhere between 10 billion and 40 billion US dollars.[41] While climate change is going to affect all of us, the reality is that developing countries, which are more heavily dependent on agriculture and natural resources, are particularly vulnerable to the impacts of rising sea levels, drought and flooding and the increased frequency and intensity of natural disasters.

Climate change has become an issue of social justice.[42] The food security of families and communities in developing countries living off the land – subsistence farmers – is extremely vulnerable to changes in weather patterns. It is vital that the international community help protect the economic development of poorer nations most vulnerable to climate change.

Whether we see it as an act of mercy, or an act of justice on a 'polluter pays' basis, in our global village developed countries will need to provide economic assistance and share technology with developing countries because the capacities of these countries to adapt are hampered by their limited human capital, technology and access to credit markets.[43]

The continual need to adapt to the intensifying impacts of climate change will pose many economic development challenges to the global community into the future.

Our Responsibility

In effect, globalization has opened our eyes to the reality of the rest of the world. The television that drones the false promises of the god of consumerism to wide-eyed Russian teenagers is the same television that projects the images of starving children and enslaved boys to our Western teens.

Desmond Tutu tells the story of how apartheid in South Africa was able to flourish in *No Future Without Forgiveness*:

> *'How was it possible for normal, decent, and God-fearing people as white South Africans considered themselves to be, to have turned a blind eye to a system which impoverished, oppressed and violated so many of those others with whom they shared the beautiful land that was their common motherland? Apartheid could not have survived for a single day had it not been supported by this enfranchised, privileged minority . . . It needs to be noted that many white people grew up knowing no other system and they acquiesced in it because it was a status quo that brought them much*

> *comfort. The system was not naïve. In fact it was exceedingly sophisticated. The black townships were usually out of sight of whites and it was an easy step from being out of sight to being out of mind. You had to put yourself to considerable inconvenience to visit a black township if you were white . . .'*[44]

The only ignorance in today's world is most often wilful. Is there a place left that does not know something of what is going on in the rest of the world? The luxury of choosing 'not to see' is now at a premium.

We are a generation saturated with more information than ever before. As a result we have subconsciously come up with a filtering mechanism to cope. We determine what we choose to absorb. If we are interested in a particular topic we learn to tune in when appropriate and then tune back out. Traditional forms of media to invoke our emotional conscience or response on an issue will not always work. This is one of the effects of globalization on social justice.

We are a generation that has been desensitized to mass suffering, because it is painful to engage in these topics and they often lead to feeling guilty about the privileges we have. Think of the famines in Ethiopia in the 1980s. Like nerve endings, tap us a few times and we react to the pain, but keep tapping and we become numb. Just watch people eating popcorn during the film *Hotel Rwanda*. Which is worse, the genocide or our ability to make it into entertainment? We are a broken and fallen world. And with all the advancements in media and communications, the coverage of suffering is unprecedented.

To choose to see and feel the pain of injustice is hard – but necessary. Unless we allow our hearts to be broken with the things that break the heart of God, our best attempts at social justice will be paternalistic and self-motivated. We will respond for ourselves, not for others. The time is coming for *real* strategies to emerge from people who will not let poverty pass them by untouched. As William Wilberforce declared, 'If to be feeling alive to all sufferings of my fellow creatures and to be warmed with the desire of relieving their distress, is to be a fanatic, I am one of the most incurable fanatics ever permitted to be at large.' Bring on the fanatics.

We want to believe this generation is the one that will change the world. The reality, of course, is that people remain wilfully ignorant. There is an incredible story and a painful vision in Ezekiel 8 and 9. God takes Ezekiel by the hair and shows him the 'terrible sin in the house of Israel'. One act at a time, God reveals sin to Ezekiel, and just when Ezekiel thinks things are as bad as they can get he is given another glimpse at even more injustice, pain and defiance against God within Israel. God sends an angel with an inkpot throughout Israel to place a mark 'on the foreheads of all who weep and sigh because of the detestable being committed in their city.' (Ezekiel 9:4 NLV) The angels coming with swords instead of inkpots later strike down any Israelite who doesn't have a mark. God is looking for people who will respond to injustice by choosing to see and then choosing to feel. We can join Bob Pierce, founder of World Vision, and pray, 'Break my heart with the things that break the heart of God.'

Glocal

On a world scale we can look at major themes of injustice such as poverty and wealth distribution, trade and globalization, HIV and AIDS, human trafficking, war, refugees and asylum seekers, reconciliation, global debt and climate change/ environment.

In *Be a Hero*, Campbell and Court take an intense look at 'seven deadly sins' of injustice facing children in the world today.[45] These seven deadly sins 'are not things of which people are guilty, but things of which they are victims'.

1. Dirt poor
2. Children in chains (child labour)
3. Orphans of the street
4. Sex and the city (sex industry, child prostitution, human trafficking)
5. AIDS and plagues
6. War-affected children
7. Religious persecution

They then link the injustices with individual action.

They call their readers to:

1. Pray the Bible (understand God's heart for justice)
2. Sponsor a child (become responsible for 'one'/invest in the life of a child)

3. Start/support a project working with children
4. Advocate for the 'invisible people'
5. Go on a 'hero holiday' (a mission immersion experience – see for yourself)

The writers are creating a link between injustice (particularly global injustice) and the way we live. The connection is a necessary one. That relation can be more than simply responding with resources to help the poor. Injustice is not something we fight alone within the global context. Relationship is at the heart of justice. Creating meaningful relationships with marginalized and vulnerable people, no matter where they live, will change the way we live. Global justice shifts to local responsibility.

The new word for social justice themes that are also rooted in local expressions is 'glocal'. This is the recognition that we are connected. No matter how far away extreme hunger is from our own experience, we know that people are going without the essentials every day. Children are dying in the deserts of Africa and young children are going without breakfast or lunch at the local inner-city school. To every 'massive' social justice issue there is also a local response. In other words, we can change the way we live and that change, no matter how small, can make a difference in the world.

Surely there is no injustice quite like dying of hunger, especially in light of the ample provision of food in the world. I remember turning on the television while I had a quick lunch break one day. I was eating eggs and toast, and thought I was pretty hungry. I sat down all settled and watched Anderson Cooper (the CNN reporter) being interviewed. The question was 'What stories have had the most impact on you?' and he began to talk about some coverage he did on a famine in Africa. He showed some of the documentary. In the clip he interviewed a doctor who treated children suffering with malnutrition.

I'll never forget it because the doctor described the process of dying from hunger by showing the symptoms on the child he was treating. He lifted the child's arm and showed the skin that was still on the table, 'This happens because there is not enough water in the child to keep the skin on the body,' said the doctor. So every time the child touches something or rubs up against something he/she loses their skin. He showed the child's inability to blink. There is not enough of the mineral zinc in the child's body to produce the water necessary for blinking. This means the child has no defence against flies or dirt in their eyes. They often go blind before they die of infection. The child dies a slow, painful and horrible death. Then the camera panned a whole field of graves, none of them marked, for there was no money to make a marker – a whole field of nameless faceless children who had died unnecessary deaths because they had no food.

I couldn't swallow. It's one thing to think about malnutrition and the deaths caused by hunger and a whole other thing to watch how that death happens. To understand the slow and painful process that could be stopped with some basic food is to feel a big pit growing in the bottom of your own stomach. The eggs turned to stone. I couldn't eat. I couldn't eat because something was terribly wrong with the world. It was injustice. I felt it. – Danielle

We ask how and why these injustices can be reality. We can see the injustice, but the causes run deep. At the heart of it is a complex layering of causes: local unemployment, drought, struggling economies in a global system that protects the interests of the wealthiest at the expense of the poor. Glocal issues have glocal solutions. We are connected to the problem and to the answers.

A Global Church

The Christian church is a global movement. Almost every Christian movement understood that God's Kingdom was meant to expand and invade the systems of the whole world. General Evangeline Booth of The Salvation Army penned the words, 'The world for God'. C.T. Studd wrote, 'Some want to live within the sound of church and chapel bell. I want to run a rescue shop within a yard of hell.'

If anything characterized the early Christian spirit, it was a global advance. Jesus himself charged his disciples to be witnesses to the ends of the earth (Acts 1:8). He saw his disciples as 'world-changers' whose lives would bring about the transformation of the whole earth. This of course, was matched to their theology. They were a people who believed in the imminent return of Christ and the coming judgement.

C.S. Lewis wrote in *Mere Christianity* 'If you read history you will find that Christians who did the most for the present world were those who thought the most of the next. It is since Christians have largely ceased to think of the other world that they have become so ineffective in this.'

Recently a professor lecturing on William Wilberforce (the English abolitionist), suggested that if Wilberforce were alive today we would label him a narrow-minded fundamentalist and relegate him to an American platform of a revivalist preacher. Largely, Wilberforce did what he did because he believed wholeheartedly in 'judgement'. He understood that Jesus was coming back and would judge us. Our gifts, our money, our time and our efforts were for something other and bigger than ourselves. We were given them in order to use them for the benefits of the Kingdom of God. This understanding shapes how we live.

When Wilberforce started 'seeing' the evil of the slave trade it had a similar effect as when William Booth 'saw' the plight of the poor in the East End of London and Elizabeth Fry first visited a women's prison – it started a fight. All of their energy, means and privilege were spent for those who had none. Gifts were not given to be squandered, but used for the expansion of the Kingdom. Catherine Booth put her children to bed at night by telling them that they were born to change the world. She didn't just want them to be happy; she wanted them to be global citizens advancing the Kingdom of God. This understanding was embedded into a Christian work ethic with social justice implications. To be a Christian means we have been called to change the world.

True biblical Christianity is not just a church with a social conscience, but a movement of people on the advance with the Kingdom of God. Social justice is not a by-product of Christian faith; they are one and the same. Reading stories of early Christians seeking to change the world through initiatives such as trade unions, job creation, political reform and the end of slavery, it is easy to see that we don't exist to simply build worshipping congregations but to change the world.

Now the challenge is to use the opportunities of globalization to help us maximize the impact for long-term social justice. The challenge and opportunity of globalization for the Christian church is to harness its energy and use it to change the world.

We contend that the scope of a movement like Christianity can thrive through globalization; it isn't a threat, it's a blessing. Now, more than ever before, our work can be connected through relationships. The power of connecting intimately through a common movement in a global context is an incredible witness to the world of what a global village could achieve. There are amazing stories of believers demonstrating to the world how we can break down issues of discrimination and prejudice of 'the other'. Christ calls us to model a different way, for he is a relational God. We are not just connected as citizens in a global community but as Christian soldiers in an advancing army. As we start to fight global issues such as human trafficking, we are in the incredible position of having a voice everywhere. As a global community, we are also locally present.

Prayer
May you have ears to hear what the Lord is saying and eyes to see what the Lord is doing. May you have a mind to learn what the Lord is teaching and a heart to love the Lord and your neighbour as yourself. Amen.

A DRUM MAJOR FOR RIGHTEOUSNESS

The Autobiography of Martin Luther King Jr. (pp.365-366)
Every now and then I guess we all think realistically about that day when we will be victimized with what is life's final common denominator – something we call death. We all think about it. And every now and then I think about my own death, and I think about my own funeral. And I don't think of it in a morbid sense.

Every now and then I ask myself, 'What is it that I would want said?' And I leave the work to you this morning. I'd like somebody to mention that day, that Martin Luther King, Jr. tried to give his life serving others. I'd like for somebody to say that day, that Martin Luther King, Jr. tried to love somebody. I want you to say that day, that I tried to be right on the war question. I want you to be able to say that day, that I did try to feed the hungry. And I want you to be able to say that day, that I did try, in my life, to visit those who were in prison. I want you to say that I tried to love and serve humanity.

Yes, if you want to say that I was a drum major, say that I was a drum major for justice. Say that I was a drum major for peace. I was a drum major for righteousness. And all of the other shallow things that will not matter. I won't have any money to leave behind. But I just want to leave a committed life behind. And that's all I wanted to say.

If I can help somebody as I pass along, if I can cheer somebody with a word or song, if I can show somebody he's travelling wrong, then my living will not be in vain. If I can do my duty as a Christian ought, if I can bring salvation to a world once wrought, if I can spread the message as the master taught, then my living will not be in vain.

MAKE POVERTY HISTORY

Nelson Mandela, 2005

As long as poverty, injustice and gross inequality persist in our world, none of us can truly rest. Massive poverty and obscene inequality are such terrible scourges of our times – times in which the world boasts breathtaking advances in science, technology, industry and wealth accumulation – that they have to rank alongside slavery and apartheid as social evils.

The Global Campaign for Action Against Poverty can take its place as a public movement alongside the movement to abolish slavery and the international solidarity against apartheid.

And I can never thank the people of Britain enough for their support through those days of the struggle against apartheid. Many stood in solidarity with us, just a few yards from this spot.

Through your will and passion, you assisted in consigning that evil system forever to history. But in this new century, millions of people in the world's poorest countries remain imprisoned, enslaved, and in chains.

They are trapped in the prison of poverty.
It is time to set them free.

Like slavery and apartheid, poverty is not natural. It is man-made and it can be overcome and eradicated by the actions of human beings. And overcoming poverty is not a gesture of charity. It is an act of justice. It is the protection of a fundamental human right, the right to dignity and a decent life.

While poverty persists, there is no true freedom.

Trade Justice

The steps that are needed from the developed nations are clear. The first is ensuring trade justice.

I have said before that trade justice is a truly meaningful way for the developed countries to show commitment to bringing about an end to global poverty.

The second is an end to the debt crisis for the poorest countries. The third is to deliver much more aid and make sure it is of the highest quality.

In 2005, there is a unique opportunity for making an impact.

In September, world leaders will gather in New York to measure progress since they made the Millennium Declaration in the year 2000.

That declaration promised to halve extreme poverty.

But at the moment, the promise is falling tragically behind. Those leaders must now honour their promises to the world's poorest citizens.

I say to all those leaders: do not look the other way; do not hesitate. Recognize that the world is hungry for action, not words. Act with courage and vision.

Call to Generation

. . . Sometimes it falls upon a generation to be great. You can be that great generation. Let your greatness blossom.

Of course the task will not be easy. But not to do this would be a crime against humanity, against which I ask all humanity now to rise up.

FIVE: THE THREE JUSTICES

Finding tools to 'unpack' injustice is difficult. There are many of them, but often they are complex in themselves. The Emet System provides a simple and helpful framework for a deeper grasp of oppression.[46] The framework suggests that true social justice consists of three distinct but interlinked and inseparable justices: Egalitarian, Distributive and Legislative.

We've already offered two models of response. This is another model that will help us both 'see' and, in our analysis of the context, break down complex injustices into workable pieces. Sometimes in order to get to the heart of an injustice all the layers have to be pulled back and examined.

This tri-justice model also fits with Micah 6:8.

Egalitarian Justice: walk humbly
(this is recognition of our creator who has created us in his image and therefore our brother/sister as well.)

Distributive Justice: love mercy
(to understand the generous and open-handed spirit of God Himself who has given the world more than enough to share.)

Legislative Justice: act justly
(rules and laws to establish protection and guidance in order that justice would be lived out through community.)

It's annoying but justice
and equality are mates.
Aren't they?
Justice always wants to
hang out with equality.
And equality is a real pain.

Bono 2006, National Prayer Breakfast[47]

Every group, whether it is a community, family, or a national structure, is measured by the three justices. They are deeply connected. So, when one area is violated, it impacts the other two. Likewise, when one area is improved it will improve the others. This approach is in three parts: like body, spirit and soul.

We will explore the basic concept of each section, but keep in mind that because they are three, they have to work together. No one section is the complete explanation. In justice work, people have different expertise in various areas. These can become camps that create barriers, and we assign value based on what camp we prefer. So, a lawyer may argue that legislative reform is the only way to really challenge injustice; social workers may insist that equality is the way and welfare economists might focus on redistribution. Biblical justice is a celebration of these parts working together. Micah 6:8 is a triune command from a triune God that unites our efforts as one.

To achieve true social justice, we need people advocating for all three. 'Too often we have wasted our energy being dismissive and cynical of each other's roles. We have to work together to complement each other's gifts. We have to become good listeners. We have to listen to the poor, those in hands on ministry, and those in advocacy. We have to listen to each other. If we combine our experience and gifts, then we can do great things.'[48]

The tri-justice model

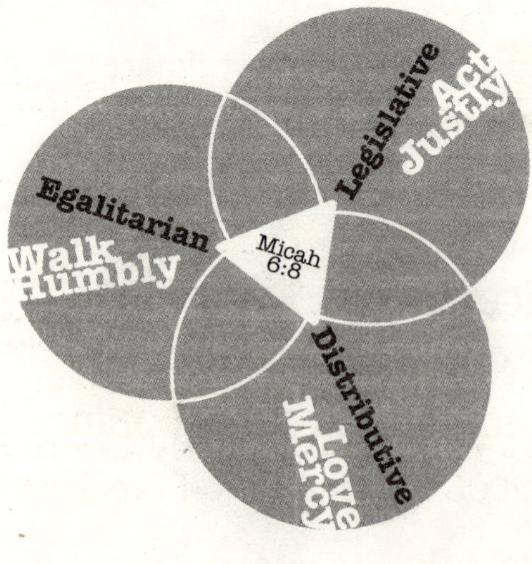

Egalitarian Justice

'So God created man in his own image,
in the image of God he created him;
male and female he created them' (Genesis 1:27)

'For you created my inmost being;
you knit me together in my mother's womb.
I praise you because I am fearfully and wonderfully made;
your works are wonderful, I know that full well.' (Psalm 139:13-14)

Imageo Deo is a Latin term meaning 'in the image of God', which the early church used to form its earliest belief statements. Every person is made in the image of God and as such has equal value. There is an intrinsic value within every person: no matter what they look like, their social class or where they are from, people are to be treated with respect and deserve equality. This means that equal treatment and respect are not based on where we're from or what we do but *who* we are: a child of God made in his image.

Egalitarian justice favours equality for all. This means equality within the system – legally, economically and socially. In the words of Mother Teresa 'There is only one God and He is God to all; therefore it is important that everyone is seen as equal before God.'

Distributive Justice

Distributive justice is concerned about a just, or fair, distribution of wealth and goods among a society. If the world were a big pie, then it ought to be cut in such a way that everyone could have a piece. For those of us who consider equality and egalitarian justice important, it is distributive justice that calls us to re-examine our excessive lifestyles in a world where people are literally dying of hunger. 'Inequality is not something that is bad in itself, but rather something that is bad in so far as it leads to oppressive relationships'.[49] Those with the largest piece of the pie have the power to rob those without of their equality. Many wars and conflicts have been centred on distributive injustice.

Distribution is central to God's Kingdom and to our discipleship. Ched Myers highlights this link through the story of the rich man in Mark's gospel:

'Who, then, can be saved?' (Mark 10:26). Mark's epilogue to the call of the rich man (Mark 10:17-25) anticipates our incredulity: Does Jesus really expect the "haves" (that is, us) to participate in Sabbath wealth redistribution[50] as a condition for discipleship? Can we imagine a world in which there are no rich and poor? To the disciples' skepticism, and to ours, Jesus replies simply: "I know it seems impossible to you, but for God all things are possible" (10:27).'[51]

For the church with a clear mandate to assist the poor, it is disturbing that 'in most churches, less than two cents of every dollar goes for overseas missions. Over 700 Protestant agencies combined had less to spend in a recent year than the potato chip budget of the US. A congregation in Texas works to match every dollar they spend on themselves with a dollar to help other people. And a congregation in South Korea commits at least 60 cents of every dollar to help other people. So most of us can do much more.'[52]

While redistribution might seem to suggest charity, distributive justice is also about preventing the gross inequality of wealth distribution within the system to begin with. While campaigns such as 'Trade Not Aid' address legislative concerns, these issues are also grounded in our individual consumer choices. We purchase, support and therefore create consumer demand for the products of companies that are exploiting the poor. We are contributing to the problem of distribution and extreme poverty. In this global system, we are all linked. An example of a campaign and action against unfair distribution and remuneration for labour is the concept of fair trade.

'The fair trade principle is an international movement that aims to ensure producers in third world countries get a fair deal for their products. Producers of crops such as coffee, tea, cocoa and rice are paid a fair price and offered long-term contracts to guarantee a sustainable livelihood. Fair trade strives for a more just distribution of revenues resulting from global trade relationships. The working and living conditions of producers and workers in economically disadvantaged regions should be improved by creating market access for their products and fair conditions. Fair trade fosters sustainable development.

It strives for social justice, economic development, environmental protection and the maintenance of cultural diversity as well as contributing to stronger trade relations between countries in the southern hemisphere.'

For more information on fair trade, visit the Fairtrade Association at www.fairtrade.org.uk

For technical information on fair trade such as fair trade standards for different products visit the international governing body, Fairtrade Labelling Organizations International (FLO) at www.fairtrade.net

Complexity of Simplicity
Shane Claiborne

'When we talk of materialism and simplicity, we must always begin with love for God and neighbour, otherwise we're operating out of little more than legalistic, guilt-ridden self-righteousness. Our simplicity is not an ascetic denunciation of material things to attain personal piety, for if we sell all that we have and give it to the poor, but have not love, it is meaningless (1 Cor. 13:3) . . . Simplicity is meaningful only inasmuch as it is grounded in love, authentic relationships, and interdependence. Redistribution then springs naturally out of our rebirth, from a vision of family that is larger than biology or nationalism. As we consider what it means to be born again into a family in which our sisters and brothers are starving to death. Then we begin to see why rebirth and redistribution are inextricably bound up in one another, as a growing number of evangelicals have come to proclaim. It also becomes scandalous for the church to spend money on windows and buildings when some family members don't have water. Welcome to the dysfunctional family of Yahweh.

So it's important to understand that redistribution comes from community, not before community. Redistribution is not a prescription for community. Redistribution is a description of what happens when people fall in love with each other across class lines. When the Bible tells the story of the early church in the book of Acts, it does not say that they were of one heart and mind because they sold everything. Rather they held all in common precisely because they were of one heart and mind, as rich and poor found themselves born again into a family in which some had extra and others were desperately in need. Redistribution was not systematically regimented but flowed naturally out of a love for God and neighbour.'[53]

Legislative Justice

> 'For our struggle is not against flesh and blood, but against the rulers, against the authorities, against the powers of this dark world' (Ephesians 6:12)

Justice is driven not only by the laws of the land but also the regulations, whether implicit or explicit, that establish what is or is not allowed. Legislative justice is therefore the establishment and upholding of laws that provide protection for those most disadvantaged in society. Martin Luther King, Jr. said, 'It may be true that the law cannot make a man love me, but it can stop him from lynching me, and I think that's pretty important.'

This is evidenced as a priority of God through the Levitical code (the 'laws' set up for Israelites to settle in their land). It included a solid framework of legislative justice to ensure equal opportunities and protection for the poor.

> 'Poverty is not a natural state of affairs, but a function of deep inequities in the national and global systems. The poor and the rich may be physically segregated from each other, but there is a systemic connection between them. Obviously, these connections are both politically and empirically complex as both poverty and inequality are multidimensional concepts and phenomena that are difficult to definite and measure.'[54]

Every society has a social agreement on which its laws are established and enforced. But it is important to recognize that not all of them are based on a 'just' framework. Many societies would have been established on slavery, for example. Often trade practices throughout history have been unjust in their outcomes. Lots of multinational corporations, despite statements of social responsibility, continue unjust practices in the name of 'progress' and are not held accountable by their stakeholders (such as their shareholders, suppliers and customers). These systems need to be exposed and challenged through solid legislative law reform.

It is important to note that legislative justice is not only about punishment or criminal justice. It is about establishing laws that protect the vulnerable. It is not just about prison time, but also about rehabilitation. It is not about retribution but restitution. It is about legislation that upholds the dignity of all persons, even those who have violated it.

An example of this is the 'John Schools' created in North America. Men who have violated the law by exploiting women through prostitution are offered the opportunity of a 'diversion' program called 'John School'. The word 'john' is slang for a prostitute's client. The program bypasses the court system, but includes a steep fine which pays for the school and exit programs for women in prostitution. It is an opportunity to learn the truth about prostitution. The perpetrators go to 'school' on a weekend and hear the testimonies of women who have suffered from being exploited. The results of the John Schools are amazing. Men who take a long hard look at prostitution through the stories of women caught in its grip rarely participate in it again. It's a legislative justice that upholds not only the letter of the law but the spirit of it as well.[55]

The Three Justices: Human Trafficking

If we use the systemic justice framework to unpack an injustice it might look something like this:

What is trafficking?
The United Nations defines it thus: 'Trafficking in human beings shall mean the recruitment, transportation, transfer, harbouring or receipt of persons, by means of the threat or use of force or other forms of coercion, of abduction, of fraud, of deception, of the abuse of power or of a position of vulnerability or of the giving or receiving of payments or benefits to achieve the consent of a person having control over another person, for the purpose of exploitation. Exploitation shall include, at a minimum, the exploitation of the prostitution of others or other forms of sexual exploitation, forced labour or services, slavery or practices similar to slavery, servitude or the removal of organs.'[56]

What is the scale of human trafficking?
Men, women and children are trafficked within their own countries and across international borders. Trafficking affects every continent and almost every country.

Due to the hidden and illegal nature of human trafficking, gathering statistics on the scale of the problem is a complex and difficult task. There are no reliable national or international estimates as to the extent of trafficking. Figures are usually counted in the countries that people are trafficked into and often fail to include those who are trafficked within their own national borders. The following statistics may represent an underestimation of trafficking, but are the most credible and frequently quoted.

- At least 12.3 million people are victims of forced labour worldwide. Of these, 2.4 million are as a result of human trafficking.[57]
- Between 600,000 and 800,000 men, women and children are trafficked across international borders each year. Approximately 80 per cent are women and girls. Up to 50 per cent are minors.[58]
- An estimated 1.2 million children are trafficked each year.[59]
- The majority of trafficked victims arguably come from the poorest countries and poorest strata of the national population.[60]
- Trafficking is the fastest growing means by which people are caught in the trap of slavery.
- Human trafficking is the third largest source of income for organized crime, exceeded only by arms and drugs trafficking.[61]
- It is the fastest growing form of international crime, already generating seven billion dollars per year in criminal proceeds. There are even reports that some trafficking groups are switching their cargo from drugs to human beings, in search of higher profits at lower risk.[62]
- People are trafficked into prostitution, begging, forced labour, military service, domestic service, forced illegal adoption, forced marriage and so on.
- Types of recruitment include: abduction, false agreement with parents, being sold by parents, runaways, the promise of travel with family, orphans sold from street or institutions.

It is obvious that human trafficking is a major injustice plaguing the world today. Like most injustices, it is complex and fraught with layers of oppression. Often people become aware and passionate about a social injustice and learn about its definitions and accompanying statistics, but then feel helpless to combat it. In order to make an impact that will help, we need to take a deeper look at the issues surrounding human trafficking.

Using the Three Justices Through a Global View

Equality

One of the main reasons human trafficking is flourishing around the world is the damaged reality of *imageo deo* (the image of God in people). Intrinsic value is not something that we can take for granted. Often cultures, economies and bottom-line profits have reduced 'people' to 'things'.

One of the key issues at the heart of the human slave trade is the reduction of people to 'commodities' with a monetary value. *How much for a person?* Pope John Paul II spoke prophetically on this to people around the world, 'The greatest threat to the next generation is excessive capitalism and the death of children not yet born.'[63] This suggests the problem inherent in human trafficking is much deeper than it appears. A society that insists people are disposable commodities is in danger of excessive exploitation.

Human trafficking is essentially revisiting the slave trade all over again. The trade flourished because people convinced themselves that 'black' people weren't the same as 'white' people. Although it can be difficult to admit, people who are different to us are often treated that way as well. Victor Malarek in *The Natashas* writes 'While it's difficult to comprehend the wall of complacency trafficked women face each and every day, there is an ugly reality behind it – racism.'[64] This can be in attitude or in laws, and is most often gender-based. More than 80 per cent of trafficked victims are women and children. In many cultures the rights of women and children are neglected. Laws are created in many societies that force women to be subservient to and dependent on men, leaving them vulnerable to exploitation and virtually powerless to protect themselves.

This is linked to issues of gender and nationality. In his book *One World: the Ethics of Globalization*, Peter Singer talks about the discounted value we place on lives outside our national borders.

> *'We put the interests of our fellow citizens far above those of citizens of other nations, whether the reason for doing so is to avoid damaging the*

economic interests of Americans at the cost of bringing floods to the people of Bangladesh, to avoid risking the lives of NATO troops at the cost of more innocent lives in Kosovo, or to help those in need rather than those in need abroad . . .

If those "at home" to whom we might give charity are already able to provide their basic needs, and seem poor only relative to our own high standards of living, is the fact that they are our compatriots sufficient to give them priority over others with greater needs? Asking these questions leads us to consider to what extent we really can, or should, make "one world" a moral standard that transcends the nation-state.'[65]

Ultimately, walking humbly requires us to treat others, no matter what their culture, as sacred. They are also made in the image of God and worthy of dignity and respect. Jesus laid this out clearly in the two greatest commandments, summing up the law with 'Love your neighbour as yourself.' Our neighbours include people different to ourselves. They include the women and children (and sometimes men) caught in the injustice of human trafficking. They are our sisters and brothers in Christ, made in the image of God.

Distribution

Extreme poverty is one of the major factors contributing to human trafficking. 'Economic need is often the condition that paves the way for human trafficking. Every year, hundreds of thousands of people respond to what they believe are economic opportunities in a distant urban centre or another country. They venture out on what they expect to be a one-year contract to perform cleaning services or factory work but are lured into a trafficking scheme that relegates some of them to prostitution and others to remote labour environments.'[66]

Poverty leaves people despairing and without hope. This is often associated with a breakdown in community that traffickers exploit – situations where individuals can't turn to family, friends and the community for support. Desperate people do desperate things like selling their children or themselves in the frantic hope of survival. People are willing to risk all to be part of the great life they 'see' in the Western world.

In some ways our heritage in the Western world is similar. Many of our great-grandparents risked everything on the hope of a new life in a new world. We are the beneficiaries of helpful immigration policies that saw the need to spread resources and opportunities. The church was involved in relocating hundreds of thousands of immigrants from England to new countries in the early 1900s. Part of the vision for social reform was relocating people to colonies and teaching them to work the land, thereby providing them with opportunities to defeat extreme poverty.

Today immigration requirements are based on the perceived needs of the host country. As a result they are often biased against the people most in need. Poor women and children are the least likely to be able to access the legal possibility of a new life. This leaves them even more susceptible to the illegal trade in humans. Even in nations where prostitution has been legalized most of the women surveyed would get out of it if they thought they could make a living any other way.

Donna Hughes reports:

> *'In contrast to many myths and misconceptions about prostitutes, women do not want to be in prostitution. A 1998 study on the sex industries in Indonesia, Malaysia, the Philippines, and Thailand found that 96 percent of those interviewed would leave prostitution if they could. A nine-country (Canada, Columbia, Germany, Mexico, South Africa, Thailand, Turkey, United States, and Zambia) study of 854 individuals in prostitution found that 89 percent of them wanted to escape prostitution. A 1995 study of women in prostitution in San Francisco reported that 88 percent of 130 women interviewed wanted to get out of prostitution. These research findings overwhelmingly demonstrate that women on every continent want to be free of prostitution.'*[67]

Selling your body, your children, your future and your life is not a decision made when you have other viable choices. Extreme poverty creates a vacuum that only redistribution can fill.

Legislative

Often laws do not exist to adequately protect children and women from the sex trade. In some countries, tourism has been established around the 'selling of women and children' for the pleasure of visiting Western men. Many business trips are offered in Asia for this reason. Furthermore, even if laws to protect the vulnerable do exist, they are rarely enforced and tragically police can sometimes be complicit in the illegal trade.[68]

'Corrupt police systems around the world also contribute to the problem. There are numerous documented cases of police officers being bribed to pick up people in a supposed raid. Some of these individuals are never booked – they just disappear without a witness or a word. They are shipped to a remote farm or other location, where they live out the rest of their lives in an environment that is entirely foreign to them. Sometimes, they can't even understand the language. All they know is that if they don't do a solid 14-hour day at the place they have been taken, they will be punished.' [69]

People get caught in human trafficking through what can be categorized as push and pull factors. Things that push people into slavery include extreme poverty. Things that pull people into slavery include enticing advertisements that suggest economic security through a job in the West. Biased immigration laws are a significant push factor that contributes to illegal movement of persons. But there are many more legislative issues surrounding human trafficking that perpetuate this particular injustice.

The International Justice Mission was born out of a desire to uphold and institute legislative reform to provide justice for the victims of trafficking around the world. The Vice President of Government Relations with the International Justice Mission, Holly J. Burkhalter, testified before the US senate in Washington in 2007:

'Today, slavery is illegal virtually everywhere. Yet this most durable of crimes against humanity continues. Millions of women, men and children suffer a daily physical reality of forced labour and lives of the bleakest misery . . . Members of the United States Senate and the House of Representatives in our day have already risen to the challenge of abolishing in fact as well as law the violent, degrading, injurious, unpaid, forced, and coerced conditions of labour at home and abroad . . . The authors of the Millennium Challenge Act conditioned access to large amounts of foreign assistance to meeting a standard of good governance that included an end to corruption – a key factor in the existence of slavery today. While these and other statutes might be improved by various amendments and excisions, the most difficult and significant work for this Congress is to insist on the execution of existing law that we have in our hands . . . If supported and enforced, these laws could contribute substantially towards the abolition of these crimes in our lifetime.' [70]

In developed nations we have legislative shortcomings as well. In many Western countries today, victims of human trafficking face the real possibility of being arrested, detained and then deported. Treated as criminals, they are re-victimized and returned to desperate situations, turned away by a legislative system that refuses to protect them.

> 'In a typical brothel raid or street sweep in cosmopolitan cities throughout the world, foreign prostitutes are rounded up and charged. For the most part, the authorities don't treat these women as victims of crime; they are regarded simply as illegal migrants. No attempt is made to determine whether they were trafficked. They are jailed, processed for immigration or labour violations and deported as quickly as possible. Innocent women, in other words, are stigmatized and then victimized over and over again.'[71]

The survivors of human trafficking are only the beginning of legislative justice; even deeper injustices are found in the societal views and demand for sex. A paper by Hughes, Carlson and Carlson from the University of Rhode Island proposes three main components to the demand for commercial sex:

1. The primary level component being the men (and occasional women) who seek out women, children and sometimes men, to purchase sex acts – these are the clients, also commonly referred to as 'johns'. Without them making the decision to buy sex acts, prostitution would not exist.
2. The profiteers of the sex industry, those who make a profit by meeting the demand – these are the traffickers, pimps, brothel owners, corrupt officials, and so on.
3. The culture that indirectly creates a demand for victims by normalizing prostitution. The media glamorizes public opinions of sex such as stripping and lap dancing which usually overlook the violence and victimization involved in the exploitation and abuse of victims of the global sex trade.

'All of these factors are supported by cultural attitudes that relegate women and girls to second-class status in society. In places where women and girls or certain ethnicities or classes of women and girls are devalued, there is more acceptance of prostitution and the exploitation of a female relative in prostitution to financially support the family.'[72]

Action Plan

Understanding oppression should lead to strategies for action. These strategies are not answers but the beginning of the journey toward solutions. Often, it's only when we take the first steps towards a solution that the larger strategy emerges.

After unpacking some of the oppression behind human trafficking, what is an appropriate response?

As we have said before, because our world is linked, the response is both global and local – it's 'glocal'. Depending on context, our responses will differ. One example of a widespread global awareness campaign is Stop The Traffik.[73] For a local assault against human traffickers check out the UK-based Croydon Community Against Trafficking.[74] There are many more. It's important to realize that people and communities have the capacity to fight injustice in their own context. We need to journey with people in order to help them recognize their own voice and gifts and use them. Those working locally in a developing country can ask how we can build a community's capacity to respond in a village where families have been prey to traffickers. One successful initiative in the Philippines has been to teach local villagers how to spot a trafficker. They are empowered to deny the trafficker the right to exploit their young people. It is important we build healthy communities that work together to strengthen people to help prevent and fight injustice.

A glocal response can range from general advocacy and awareness to specific, intentional interventions. A person in a financially-secure home, living in a seemingly secure neighbourhood may enter the social justice fight by choosing to become aware of human trafficking and then spreading that awareness within their sphere of influence. That's a genuine and good response. Another may choose to find the local brothels hidden in the fabric of their neighbourhood, or one close by, and confront the injustice head-on, as the community in Croydon did. And yet another may choose to sponsor an asylum seeker and use their extra bedroom to house a global neighbour at risk.

One person may respond to extreme poverty by contributing to income-generating projects (i.e. loaning interest-free capital to women in the developing world). Another may feel compelled to go to a developing country and facilitate economic models and train local leaders to administer the program. And yet another may choose to confront the excesses of materialism in their own life and live simply, or realize they've objectified women and choose to confront and change their beliefs and behaviours. All are good responses. All are necessary. All of these responses are rooted in a deep understanding of this injustice, both its root causes and potential long-term solutions.

What follows is a brainstorming exercise exploring the potential strategies that emerge after a systemic framework analysis.

EQUALITY

AWARENESS ABOUT GENDER INEQUALITY:

> Promotions for equality/human rights around the globe
> Treating women and children with respect
> Empowering women and children
> Creating equal opportunity for economic security[75]
> Teaching theology on gender equality[76]
> Exposing prejudices regarding people and race
> Not tolerating inequality
> Speaking up

'Study after study has taught us that there is no tool for development more effective than the empowerment of women. No other policy is likely to raise economic productivity, or to reduce infant and maternal mortality. No other policy is as sure to improve nutrition and promote health—including the prevention of HIV/AIDS. No other policy is as powerful in increasing the chances of education for the next generation.'—Kofi Annan, United Nations Secretary-General, International Women's Day 2005

STOP SEXUAL OPPRESSION (PORNOGRAPHY AND SEXUAL VIOLENCE)[77]

Equality is a fierce commitment to the rights of every person – treating people from all walks of life and circumstances with respect. It is a determination to know people different from us and celebrate the differences. It's an awareness of human rights violations around the world and doing something about it. For example, Amnesty International started when one man became aware of an unjust prison sentence and has become a global advocacy group!

PERSONAL REFLECTION QUESTIONS

Do I treat all people as equal?

How many people unlike me do I even know by name?

Who is being treated unfairly in my community?

Who is being treated unfairly in the world?

How am I contributing to the equality of persons?

What are my views on sex?

Do I see prostituted persons as objects that can be bought?

DISTRIBUTION

What are your views on money and wealth?

We met a family who had taught their children that everything they had belonged to Jesus and He was simply letting us use it. This was great stewardship teaching for young kids. We liked it so much we started to teach our son the same thing. I wasn't sure he was catching on until one day he was jumping on the bed and I told him, 'Stop jumping on my bed!' to which he replied, 'It's not your bed, it's Jesus'!' And he's right. A 'me' culture can only hope to widen the gap between the 'haves' and the 'have nots'. In order to fight this rugged individualistic, wealth-saturated cultural reality we have to get fierce with our generosity.

Danielle

SOLUTIONS TO EXTREME POVERTY:

> Financial resources such as micro-credit.

> Exit strategies for women and children caught in oppression (rehabilitation centres that offer job training for survivors who need other employment options).

> Provision for the survivors of trafficking. UN Palermo Protocol outlines the basic needs.

> Join in a campaign calling your government and governments around the world to uphold the promises of the protocol.

> Join larger campaigns such as Make Poverty History, ONE and Stop The Traffik.

> Share your own resources

> Challenge your church to give more to developing world projects.

PERSONAL REFLECTION QUESTIONS

How much of my expendable income do I spend on my family or myself?

How much of my personal wealth do I contribute to the developing world?

How much of my business? Am I open-handed with my things?

Do I pray about the money I spend?

LEGISLATIVE

- Join a campaign placing pressure on countries to uphold and enforce the law regarding human trafficking, including stiff penalties for those who break it and re-training and provision for the victims of it.
- Trafficking visa reform in developed countries. This will ensure that victims of trafficking aren't treated as criminals because of immigration regulations. There needs to be a protective legislation that ensures that survivors can access the provision they need to recover and not be re-victimized and/or re-trafficked.
- General immigration reform.
- Welcoming communities. Asylum seekers need support that goes beyond legislation. One of the ways we can help in the process is by becoming sponsors to refugees.
- Pressuring national governments to uphold promises and laws.[78]
- Prostitution and human trafficking are linked. Inform yourself about the alternative solutions to prostitution in a society. Sweden offers one model (see chapter six) and there are others. Get informed and then become an advocate for a just solution.
- Get to know the people who are 'weak' and despised, forgotten and oppressed.
- Becoming a 'learner' of the poor.[79] Knowing them will help you understand unjust legislation.

PERSONAL REFLECTION QUESTIONS

How many petitions have I signed in order to change an unjust law?

Am I aware of legislative reforms needed in my country?

Do I know the concerns of the 'poor' in my own neighbourhood or city?

Have I ever met a prostituted person?

Would I consider sponsoring an asylum seeker?

Prayer

Let us go out from our customs and our habits and
learn to hope from the Bible.
Let us go out and cross the frontiers so that we may
infect life with hope.
Let us ignore the barriers, and look only to the
One who breaks them down.
He is risen. Jesus is risen indeed.
Blessed be the Lord for ever and ever.

REMARKS BY BONO

Receiving the Chairman's Award at the 38th NAACP Image Awards [80]
(Los Angeles, CA, March 2, 2007)

You see, I grew up in Ireland, when Ireland was divided along religious lines, sectarian lines. Young people like me were parched for the vision that poured out of the pulpits of black America, and the vision of a black Reverend from Atlanta . . . A man who refused to hate because he knew love would do a better job.

These ideas travel, you know. And they reached me clear as any tune, lodged in my brain like a song. I couldn't shake that. This was Ireland in the 70s growing up . . . And people like me looked across the ocean to the NAACP. And I'm here tonight and that feels good. It feels very, very good.

Well today the world looks again to the NAACP. We need the community that taught the world about civil rights to teach it something about human rights. I'm talking about the right to live like a human. The right to live, period. Those are the stakes in Africa right now.

Five and a half thousand Africans dying every day of AIDS – a preventable, treatable disease. Nearly a million Africans, most of them children, dying every year from malaria – death by mosquito bite. This is not about charity, as you know here in this room. This is about justice. It's about justice and equality.

Now I know that America hasn't solved all of its problems. I know AIDS is still killing people right here in America. And I know the hardest hit are African Americans, many of them young women. Today at a church in Oakland I went to see such extraordinary people. This lioness here, Barbara Lee, took me around with her pastor, J. Alfred Smith. And may I say that it was the poetry and the righteous anger of the black church that was such an inspiration to me, a very white – almost pink – Irish man, growing up in Dublin.

This is true religion. True religion will not let us fall asleep in the comfort of our freedom. Love thy neighbor is not a piece of advice. It's a command. And that means a lot. That means a lot. That means that in the global village we're gonna have to start loving a whole lot more people – that's what that means. His truth is marching on.

Two million Americans have signed up to the ONE campaign to make poverty history. Tonight the NAACP is signing up to work with us. And so can you. His truth is marching on.

Because where you live should not decide whether you live or whether you die. And to those in the church who still sit in judgement on the AIDS emergency, let me climb into the pulpit for just one moment. Because whatever thoughts we have about God, who he is or even if God exists, most will agree that God has a special place for the poor.

The poor are where God lives.

God is in the slums, in the cardboard boxes where the poor play house. God is where the opportunity is lost and lives are shattered. God is with the mother who has infected her child with the virus that will take both their lives. God is under the rubble and the cries we hear during war time.

God, my friends, is with the poor.

And God is with us, if we are with them.

This is not a burden. This is an adventure.

Don't let anyone tell you it cannot be done.

We can be the generation that ends extreme poverty.

NOBLE LECTURE

Muhammad Yunus, Oslo, December 10, 2006.[81]

Grameen Bank

Today, Grameen Bank gives loans to nearly 7 million poor people, 97 per cent of whom are women, in 73,000 villages in Bangladesh. Grameen Bank gives collateral-free income generating, housing, student and micro-enterprise loans to the poor families and offers a host of attractive savings, pension funds and insurance products for its members. Since it introduced them in 1984, housing loans have been used to construct 640,000 houses. The legal ownership of these houses belongs to the women themselves. We focused on women because we found giving loans to women always brought more benefits to the family.

In a cumulative way the bank has given out loans totalling about US $6 billion. The repayment rate is 99 per cent. Grameen Bank routinely makes profit. Financially, it is self-reliant and has not taken donor money since 1995. Deposits and own resources of Grameen Bank today amount to 143 per cent of all outstanding loans. According to Grameen Bank's internal survey, 58 per cent of our borrowers have crossed the poverty line.

Grameen Bank was born as a tiny homegrown project run with the help of several of my students, all local girls and boys. Three of these students are still with me in Grameen Bank, after all these years, as its topmost executives. They are here today to receive this honour you give us.

This idea, which began in Jobra, a small village in Bangladesh, has spread around the world and there are now Grameen-type programs in almost every country.

Second Generation

It is 30 years now since we began. We keep looking at the children of our borrowers to see what has been the impact of our work on their lives. The women who are our borrowers always gave topmost priority to the children. One of the Sixteen Decisions developed and followed by them was to send children to school. Grameen Bank encouraged them, and before long all the children were going to school. Many of these children made it to the top of their class. We wanted to celebrate that, so we introduced scholarships for talented students. Grameen Bank now gives 30,000 scholarships every year.

Many of the children went on to higher education to become doctors, engineers, college teachers and other professionals. We introduced student loans to make it easy for Grameen students to complete higher education. Now some of them have PhDs. There are 13,000 students on student loans. Over 7,000 students are now added to this number annually.

We are creating a completely new generation that will be well equipped to take their families way out of the reach of poverty. We want to make a break in the historical continuation of poverty.

We Create What We Want

We get what we want, or what we don't refuse. We accept the fact that we will always have poor people around us, and that poverty is part of human destiny. This is precisely why we continue to have poor people around us. If we firmly believe that poverty is unacceptable to us, and that it should not belong to a civilized society, we would have built appropriate institutions and policies to create a poverty-free world.

We wanted to go to the moon, so we went there. We achieve what we want to achieve. If we are not achieving something, it is because we have not put our minds to it. We create what we want.

What we want and how we get to it depends on our mindsets. It is extremely difficult to change mindsets once they are formed. We create the world in accordance with our mindset. We need to invent ways to change our perspective continually and reconfigure our mindset quickly as new knowledge emerges. We can reconfigure our world if we can reconfigure our mindset.

We Can Put Poverty in the Museums

I believe that we can create a poverty-free world because poverty is not created by poor people. It has been created and sustained by the economic and social system that we have designed for ourselves; the institutions and concepts that make up that system; the policies that we pursue.

Poverty is created because we built our theoretical framework on assumptions which underestimates human capacity, by designing concepts which are too narrow (such as concepts of business, creditworthiness, entrepreneurship, employment) or developing institutions which remain half-done (such as financial institutions, where poor are left out). Poverty is caused by the failure at the conceptual level, rather than any lack of capability on the part of people.

I firmly believe that we can create a poverty-free world if we collectively believe in it. In a poverty-free world, the only place you would be able to see poverty is in the poverty museums. When school children take a tour of the poverty museums, they would be horrified to see the misery and indignity that some human beings had to go through. They would blame their forefathers for tolerating this inhuman condition, which existed for so long, for so many people.

A human being is born into this world fully equipped not only to take care of him or herself, but also to contribute to enlarging the well being of the world as a whole. Some get the chance to explore their potential to some degree, but many others never get any opportunity, during their lifetime, to unwrap the wonderful gift they were born with. They die unexplored and the world remains deprived of their creativity, and their contribution.

Grameen has given me an unshakeable faith in the creativity of human beings. This has led me to believe that human beings are not born to suffer the misery of hunger and poverty.

To me poor people are like bonsai trees. When you plant the best seed of the tallest tree in a flower-pot, you get a replica of the tallest tree, only inches tall. There is nothing wrong with the seed you planted, only the soil-base that is too inadequate. Poor people are bonsai people. There is nothing wrong in their seeds. Simply, society never gave them the base to grow on. All it needs to get the poor people out of poverty is for us to create an enabling environment for them. Once the poor can unleash their energy and creativity, poverty will disappear very quickly.

Let us join hands to give every human being a fair chance to unleash their energy and creativity.

EQUALITY

At the Movies
The Constant Gardener

There is a scene where the character Justin is escaping a raid by violent rebels and heading for a waiting plane. With growing compassion for the plight of the local people, he wants to bring a young African girl, who is fleeing alongside him, onboard. The pilot refuses to take the girl, explaining that they are only allowed to evacuate aid workers. Desperate, Justin offers the pilot a bribe to take the child, but the man retorts that the rules are there for a reason. Justin cannot bear to leave her, pleading that there can be no rules to cover a child's life, but the pilot simply points out that when there are so many others in the same situation, he cannot make an exception for one little girl.

It is a scene of heart-wrenching inequality between those with rights in our world because of race (and wealth) and those without.

Hotel Rwanda
Mano Singham, 'Hotel Rwanda and Post-Colonial Ethnic Conflicts' [82]

There is also a powerful moment in the movie *Hotel Rwanda* where 'a foreign TV cameraman (played by Joaquin Phoenix) is at the hotel bar and asks a local journalist what the difference is between a Hutu and a Tutsi and how the conflict arose. The journalist replies that Tutsis are supposed to be taller and have narrower noses. He also says that the Belgian colonial powers favoured the Tutsi minority and groomed them into an elite. This caused resentment among the Hutu majority, who retaliated when they obtained power after independence. Two women are also seated at the bar and Phoenix asks them which ethnicity they are. One replies that she is Hutu and the other that she is Tutsi. Phoenix wonderingly muses "they could be twins." And there you have it in a nutshell. Each group of people likes to think of themselves as somehow special and invent qualities that they think distinguish themselves from other groups, however absurd or irrational the grounds for such beliefs.'

EQUALITY

SECTION THREE:
LET JUSTICE ROLL

SIX: IMAGINING A BETTER WORLD

The great social reformers are people who let justice fire their imagination and spirit into dreaming and working for a better world. Gunilla Ekberg is such a person, fearlessly campaigning for the rights of women in Sweden. She worked to end the sexual oppression of women by leading a controversial Bill through Parliament that made the purchasing of sex illegal.[83] At the height of the move, the Swedish government proclaimed on its website, 'We want the world to know that in Sweden, women and children are not for sale.' In the midst of Europe's sliding prostitution laws and reforms, one country created a completely new approach. Ekberg suggests that if we are going to change the behaviour of people and nations we need to be able to imagine a better world.

Imagine your country at its best. Would poor women have to sell their bodies several times a day in order to eat? If we take Ekberg seriously then the lack of better world systems is largely due to a lack of imagination.

Muhammad Yunus imagines a world where his grandchildren will have to visit and learn about poverty in a museum. 'For we can only build what we are able to imagine. Only if we conceptualize a world without poverty can we start to build it.'[84] William Wilberforce faced an incredible task. Some would have said it was impossible to dismantle the economic and societal norms of the slave trade in his day. He committed his life to end it because he could imagine a better world. William Booth, as he wrote *In Darkest England and the Way Out,* understood that God had another plan for society – a plan that was just, fair and held dignity for all people. He strove to live a gospel that not only imagined another world, but also brought it to life in vivid colour. These reformers of imagination inspire this book *Just Imagine*. We want to re-ignite our imaginations to dream of a better world and challenge the notion that changing the world is impossible.

David Ruis, in *The Justice God is Seeking*, says:

> *'At the core of His [Jesus'] Kingdom summons is this mind and heart-altering challenge . . .* repent, *for the Kingdom is upon you. To repent is to change your way of thinking – or more precisely to change the way you see life. The Greek is clear . . .* metanoia *(repent) means to shift the way you perceive. There is an alternative reality beyond what we see through*

> *the fallen sight of our natural eyes. There is another way to live; a way higher than the one we are comfortable in or resigned to.'*

Is it really any wonder that so many social reformers in history have been Christians? A new image of the world is so important that God doesn't leave it up to our imaginations alone. Consistently, he is helping us to imagine a world where there is no poverty; where health, healing, wholeness, fullness, restitution and liberation are a part of our everyday lives. Jesus calls us to imagine what life here on earth would be if it really were 'as it is in heaven'. (Matthew 6:10.) He invites us to pray for that very thing! The Bible has given us a blueprint to imagine a better world. Prophets spoke it, Jesus personified it, and Revelation paints a picture of a perfect and coming world.

The New Jerusalem (Revelation 21:1-4 NLT):

> 'Then I saw a new heaven and a new earth, for the old heaven and the old earth had disappeared. And the sea was also gone. And I saw the holy city, the new Jerusalem, coming down from God out of heaven like a bride beautifully dressed for her husband. I heard a loud shout from the throne, saying, "Look, God's home is now among his people! He will live with them, and they will be his people. God himself will be with them. He will wipe every tear from their eyes, and there will be no more death or sorrow or crying or pain. All these things are gone forever."'

Ekberg also asserts that if we are to imagine a better world we need to understand the nature of oppression. In order to release the prisoners, we need to understand how to unlock the prison doors.

Bramwell Booth, son of William Booth, the founder of The Salvation Army, understood this strategy well: utilizing people living closest to oppression to reach out to others still in it. This meant that those doing the work implicitly understood the systems and realities of the evil they were fighting against. When Booth and Stead set out to expose the evil of children caught in prostitution on the streets of London, they did it with their 'eyes wide open' to the system of oppression that existed. To better understand the implications and the working of the trade, they got help from a former brothel owner. They employed a Christian woman (Rebecca Jerritt) in a covert operation mission inside a brothel to collect information. Stead went undercover as a customer in order to find out more. Eventually their efforts rescued one girl, which blew the lid of secrecy off the situation and led to the national laws being changed and enforced in London.[85]

These were people dissatisfied with a simple hope and a prayer. They were committed to bringing heaven on earth and did so by taking a long, hard look at oppression. It is not easy work. Indeed, Booth, Jerritt and Stead took some hard hits in the process.[86] Yet this identification helped them to imagine and work for a better world.

In the introduction, we mentioned that Martin Luther King Jr. decided to move into a slum in Chicago. Only then did he understand the implicit oppression that the northern black community was facing. Wilberforce slept in a coffin made in the exact measurements of a slave hold in a ship. Sometimes he even wore the chains, because he wanted to understand the oppression in order to fight it effectively. Muhammad Yunus was confronted with extreme poverty during the famine of Bangladesh and it changed him forever. As the head of economics department at Chittagong University he struggled to reconcile the elegant theories of economics in light of the extreme poverty of his people. 'Suddenly, I felt the emptiness of those theories in the face of crushing hunger and poverty. I wanted to do something immediate to help people around me, even if it was just one human being, to get through another day with a little more ease.'[87]

The theories just didn't seem to be relevant or helpful in the reality of the everyday. He decided to find an answer by choosing to become a student of the poor. What emerged was a system that is now breaking the back of extreme poverty in Bangladesh and the wider world through micro-credit financing.[88] After criticizing the ineffectiveness of the World Bank in addressing poverty, Yunus was asked what he would do differently: 'If the overarching objective of the World Bank is to combat world poverty, then it seems to me the bank should move to a location where poverty is rampant. In Dhaka, the World Bank would be surrounded by human suffering and destitution. By living in close proximity with the problem, I believe the bank would solve the problem much faster and more realistically.'

World-changers understand that if imagining a better world is going to lead to the defeat of oppression, we need to know our enemy well.

Vancouver Bingo, Canada

When we were working in the downtown eastside of Vancouver (a modern ghetto of drug users confined to a ten-block radius), we were constantly wondering how we could change the neighbourhood for the better. We recognized the need to make a difference for the children who would, without good intervention, be the adults we would help later. Taking a wider look at the oppression of the whole city, we recognized that the cycle of addiction and violence started much earlier in the next suburb where kids at risk were already part of the cycle. So we started to build relationships with kids in that neighbourhood after school in the local park. We continued to pray that God would open the doors to really influence kids in that neighbourhood, and change the cycles of systemic poverty.

One day, out of the blue I received a phone call from a realtor. He had heard we were doing some 'work' in the neighbourhood and wondered if we wanted to take a look at a building available for rent. So two of us went to see it. It turns out the building was a huge hall right smack dab in the middle of the neighbourhood we had been praying and working for. We sensed the Lord in the connection and continued the conversation with the group wanting to rent us the building.

It turned out that the owners of the building were actually a non-profit community centre from the nice part of town. They had used the building for bingo nights as an income generator to build an ice rink in one of Vancouver's wealthier suburbs. Eventually, the government pulled the plug on local bingos in order to centralize gambling revenue. Now they were stuck with an empty building. As I met with the local leadership of the community group and began to explain why we were interested in that particular neighbourhood (kids at risk, poverty central, broken families, Aboriginal population, family violence . . .) it began to dawn on everyone that there was something grossly wrong with the situation. The distribution of wealth in this relationship between the owners and the community was messed up. It didn't take a rocket scientist to connect the dots as we reflected on the picture of one of the wealthiest neighbourhoods building an ice rink with money from the community most in need, by using the carrot of winning instant cash.

I later learned that all the parents who volunteered at the bingos were given a discount on the fees to the ice rink for their own kids. Before this, I had some illusions that the people in the richest neighbourhood hadn't really understood how they raised the funds. But after that conversation I knew that countless wealthy parents had actually come and helped collect the money from the poorest people in Vancouver to get the discount they didn't really need.

The meeting was a bit awkward after that. I hadn't intended on a guilt trip. But it was so obvious, so wrong, that the injustice of the situation was clear. Needless to say, the rent was cheap. And it should be. I humbly suggested that perhaps now that we understood what had really been happening over the last ten years, it was time for the wealthy community with the nice new ice rink to give back to the people who had funded it. It wasn't an easy journey and is still an ongoing one. But it highlighted to me the insane ability the wealthy have to treat the poor unjustly. And who knows, and who cares? It happens all the time.

Danielle

A study of reformers who have changed the world confirms Ekberg's ideas. We must imagine a better world and understand injustice. Jesus embodied this. He imagined and portrayed to his followers a better world: a world where slaves and masters were friends and sisters, gender didn't determine rights and distribution of wealth was just.

The frustration of injustice is that it creates situations that seem unsolvable. In Cape Town, South Africa you can go from one of the most notorious slum cities in the country to a state-of-the-art shopping centre. The shopping centre is built on a landfill project which was actually the remains of a 'coloured' community that had been bulldozed to the ground, and the inhabitants relocated, during apartheid. A visitor to the centre expressed that she felt as though everything she bought from that centre was contaminated. It was dirty by association. But would it rectify the situation if the shopping centre in Cape Town was demolished? The real gem of true social justice is an acknowledgment that our world is broken. Even if poor kids could shop for free it could never undo the hurt, suffering, and generational damage done. But what can be done is to take the present day realities created by past mistakes, and imagine how they can be different.

Often what blocks us from being able to imagine a better world is the inability to forgive, not only individually but corporately.

The Truth and Reconciliation Commission was instrumental in bringing about peace and reconciliation in South Africa after the apartheid. In the foreword to R.T. Kendall's book, *Total Forgiveness*, Professor Washington Okumu talks about the need for nations 'to forgive each other for their past exploitation and suppression of their weaker neighbours just as much as individuals need to do'[89] and advocates for mediation and a 'policy of reconciliation, forgiveness and restorative justice and not just retributive justice'.[90] He goes on to say: 'Bitterness, however justified, will just consume our souls and achieve nothing. We must, therefore, learn to forgive even if we don't forget. Nelson Mandela is perhaps the best example in the twentieth century of a man who has taught us how to forgive. After 27 years of political incarceration – the longest-serving political prisoner in the world – he emerged unscathed and told his people to forgive their former white oppressors and instead fix their attention on the future: on building a new united nation. In spite of the devastating trauma of Apartheid, Mandela chose the path of forgiveness and reconciliation rather than the policy of revenge and vindictiveness . . .' [91]

This was the great question of South Africa's Truth and Reconciliation Commission: we know it's been unfair, unjust and just plain wrong, but what now? Do we seek revenge or work towards forgiveness and restorative justice together?

Brad Jersak says:

'Prophetic peacemaking is restoring *shalom* wherever it has been lost or broken:

- Between God and people (reconciliation)
- Between one person or people and another (mediation)
- Between people and themselves (healing)
- Between people and creation (environmentalism)'[92]

It is the prophetic imagining of a healed world.

Worship

Worship plays an essential part in our ability to conceive of a different world and find the power to forgive while facing the realities of present injustices, because it requires significant spiritual sustenance. Worship not only sustains the fight for justice, but at its best it consistently keeps before us the vision and dream of a better world. Good worship fires our imagination. God instructs 'true' worship in scripture, and we offer it in the grit and grime of everyday living, acting justly, loving mercy and walking humbly. But it can also be celebrated and cultivated through collective worship.

Bono, the lead singer of U2, was once asked if he'd ever leave rock music to become a politician. He replied, 'Well, a speech can really impact you – but a song, that becomes a part of you.' The impact of music has been felt in every social reform. *Amazing Grace* is a great example of the clarion call of transformation, offering hope for the slave and the slave-trader alike. Slaves used gospel songs as a way of keeping hope alive in desperate situations and reminding themselves of the biblical vision of the future. *We Shall Overcome* was the theme song of the civil rights movement. Worship as a tool for re-imagining is a common theme in scripture as well. The Israelites often sang in celebration of victory and in declaration of its inevitability. The Psalmist put every justice thought and injustice tension into song and sang them publicly. They were often sung as corporate worship songs.

Psalm 137 explains the pain of trying to re-imagine the Kingdom in captivity:

> 'By the rivers of Babylon we sat and wept when we remembered Zion. There on the poplars we hung our harps, for there our captors asked us for songs, our tormentors demanded songs of joy; they said, "Sing us one of the songs of Zion!"
>
> How can we sing the songs of the LORD while in a foreign land?
>
> If I forget you, O Jerusalem, may my right hand forget its skill.
>
> May my tongue cling to the roof of my mouth if I do not remember you, if I do not consider Jerusalem my highest joy.'

Is it any wonder we've lost our prophetic imagination when our current worship is almost always individually focused? Our songs are often about feeling emotional faith in a personal relationship with God, which is why they are sometimes called 'boyfriend songs'. Contemporary worship is almost completely devoid of justice language or justice issues.

Walter Brueggemann outlines what can happen when the Christian community begins to believe the alternative reality of the Kingdom, 'a community rooted in energizing memories and summoned by radical hopes is a curiosity and a threat in current culture . . . the church has no business more pressing than the reappropriation of its memory in its full power and authenticity.'[93]

Living counter-cultural lives is at the root of justice. It's telling an established unjust system that there is another way to live, not just with words but with our lives. Sustaining the vision of this alternative reality is essential through intentional divine sustenance, through worship. We remember 'Zion' (the promised presence of God) by singing the songs of Zion. What better way to imagine the Kingdom of God coming with justice than to sing about it?

The challenge for us is to rediscover the prophetic imagination and the great songs of justice through our corporate worship. The Micah Challenge 'Heart Life Voice' project was created because songs have the power to inspire and challenge us. 'Heart Life Voice is an album of worship that speaks of God's compassion for the hungry, the poor, and the marginalized. The songs on this album challenge us to live out our faith radically through our speaking, giving, praying and doing. Heart Life Voice is a prophetic call for justice. Your church should be singing these songs.' This Kingdom imagination is awakening, echoing the cry of believers gone before. One featured song by Nathan Rowe, entitled *Let Justice Roll*, puts it like this:

> There's a river that is flowing
> Full of mercy, justice and grace
> From the Father to the nations
> Every colour, every race.
>
> Who will live, untainted by this world?
> Who will die for the gospel of our King?
> Who will hear the weeping of our Lord?
> He calls . . .
>
> Who will be my hands and feet?
> To the lost, the last, the least?
> Who will stand? Who will go?
> Who will walk this world in white?
> Who will take a stand and fight?
> Who will stand? Who will go?
> Let justice roll.[94]

The image of the Kingdom coming is one that will impact us but one that will also become part of us. The ethos of God's world emerging is something worth living for. Once we have the vision we recognize what we are aiming at. To simply imagine it will not be enough. Our imagination compels us to help make it a reality and work towards achieving the vision. William Wilberforce did just this:

> *'To fathom the magnitude of what Wilberforce did we have to see that the "disease" he vanquished forever was actually neither the slave trade nor slavery. Slavery still exists around the world today, in such measure as we can hardly fathom. What Wilberforce vanquished was something even worse than slavery, something that was much more fundamental and can hardly be seen from where we stand today; he vanquished the very mind-set that made slavery acceptable and allowed it to survive and thrive for millennia. He destroyed an entire way of seeing the world, one that had held sway from the beginning of history, and he replaced it with another way of seeing the world. Included in the old way of seeing things was the idea that the evil of slavery was good. Wilberforce murdered that old way of seeing things, and so the idea that slavery was good died along with it . . . the idea that slavery is inextricably intertwined with human civilization, and part of the way things are supposed to be, and economically necessary and morally defensible, is gone.'*[95]

Prayer

Rise up with Christ into a new day, a new life;
because for anyone who is in Christ, there is a new creation.
The old has gone and the new is here.
Therefore, go forth in joy. Amen.

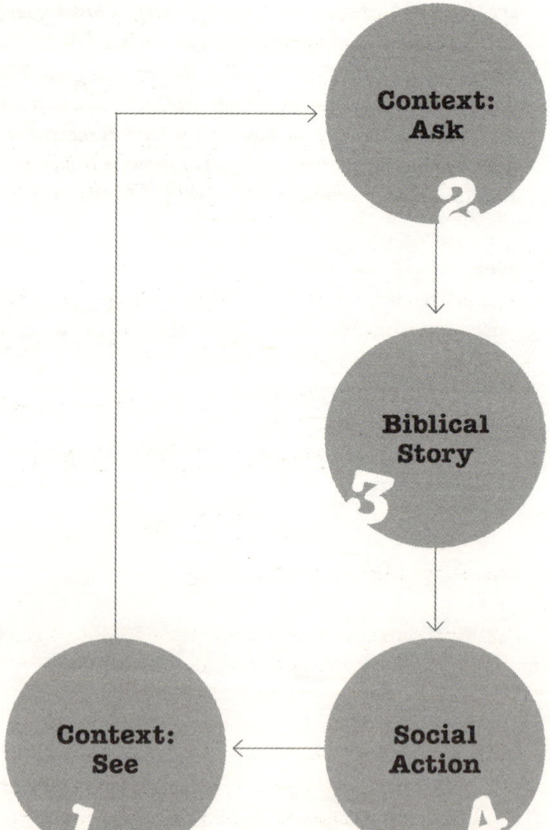
Context: Ask
2
Biblical Story
3
Social Action
4
Context: See
1

SEVEN: PROPHETIC RESPO

The modern generation has been massively influenced by prophetic voices like Martin Luther King, Jr., Nelson Mandela and others who have asked big questions and were involved in real change. But the prophetic work of the church in our generation cannot be left to the 'big prophetic voices': it needs the prophetic involvement of every Christian. To see what is required, it is helpful to look at the biblical prophets. From this four principles emerge:

1. Prophets comprehend context. They always hear and understand the plight of people.
2. Prophets analyse the situation. They continually ask why.
3. Prophets bring a God perspective. They are God-led people, seeking God's perspective on every circumstance.
4. Prophets identify action. Their understanding and analysis always leads to a call for action.

To understand our role in a biblical prophetic ministry within the contemporary world we need to undertake these four steps.

Understanding Context: Seeing

Biblical prophets start by sitting among the people, feeling their pain and understanding the nature of their lives. Their model is the God of the Exodus.

> The Lord said, 'I have indeed seen the misery of my people in Egypt. I have heard them crying out because of their slave drivers, and I am concerned about their suffering. So I have come down to rescue them from the hand of the Egyptians.' (Exodus 3:7-8, TNIV)

Jeremiah, Isaiah, and Amos all knew what the people were feeling and the injustice that affected them because they lived among them. Most effective prophetic work is done when we live in areas where our neighbours and street friends are people suffering injustice. When we see their tears and feel their anger or see their depression at the times they are treated unjustly, our sense of justice needing to be done is fired up.[96]

To the prophets, God was not a distant, remote or presidential God, but a God who lived among his people. The prophets knew they needed to see, hear and feel the sufferings of those they lived with. When we are in the context and feeling the pain of people, we start experiencing the heart of God. It is only when we empathize with the pain of others that a passion for action starts to arise in us. God's tears become our tears, God's love for people becomes our love for people, and the outrage God feels against those things that crush his children kindles our anger to subvert and change those systems. Social justice is not about professional detachment and managed relationships, it is about seeing the pain of the world as God sees it and experiences it. It's where injustice impacts us and the pain becomes personal. Sitting in the context of injustice is not easy, because the evil is so overwhelming. Often all we can do is call out to God in desperation.

This happens to Moses. When God confronted Moses he told him that he had heard the cry of his people in Egypt and asked Moses to do something. Moses, overwhelmed, tries to get out of the responsibility. He does what we often do – he gave excuses for not being involved. 'I can't speak and the Israelites won't listen. Who am I to go and represent you the almighty God, Yahweh?' Eventually, Moses' response causes God's anger to flare, because God cannot stand inaction and abdication. He isn't fond of excuses when it comes to tackling injustice.

When we start considering injustice in the context of our lives we are going to be confronted with discrimination, racism, injustice, corrupt structures and unhealthy cultural practices that leave us thinking 'Who are we to change the status quo? What can I do to change the situation?' Like Moses we may be inclined to offer the Lord and the oppressed a similar argument, 'Who am I to do something? I'm not a person of influence or authority. I can't change things. I'm not a social worker, political lobbyist, doctor, or teacher. I don't have the skill set necessary.' We can try all these arguments. God usually finds the arguments deficient.

In the end Moses relents and obeys God – not just out of duty, but because he remembered the oppression of people and the tears in their eyes. He remembers what he had seen as a young man growing up in

Egypt; the oppression, the unfairness and the exploitation of his family, tribe and nation. So Moses relents and takes up God's invitation to take the journey into justice.

Understanding Context: Asking

When we start to really see and experience the injustice around us, it leads to the necessity to ask deeper questions.

In many Western countries, indigenous peoples have high rates of imprisonment, addiction, poverty, child abuse and unemployment. We can see this and be tempted to immediately blame the victim rather than to ask more fundamental and searching questions.

History clearly shows that when a group of people are deprived of their land, culture, people and children, the effect on their social and economic wellbeing is dramatic. To control their use of alcohol or restrict their rights often leads to further problems. In many countries, indigenous people groups were alienated from their land as a result of colonization. Today they are over-represented in the social deprivation, crime, poor housing and economic deprivation statistics. In considering the social and economic plight of indigenous people groups in countries around the world, it is necessary to analyse and understand the long-term effects land and cultural alienation have had.

Analysis is needed because the obvious can be misleading. Analysis means that we ask questions when we see that people are experiencing injustice and deprivation. In the ocean a disturbance on the surface of the water is usually caused by an object or an occurrence under the surface. Likewise, where there are disturbances in our community the causes are often under the surface. Analysis tries to understand what that underlying cause or problem is.

For example, a client requested food assistance from a local food-bank. Checking on the background of the person seeking assistance, the worker discovered that the family had been the victims of the activities of a rogue car dealer. The car dealer fraudulently sold them a damaged vehicle using their house as security. After only two weeks of driving the car, it needed a costly engine overhaul and the family were unable to meet the car payments. The dealer promptly put their house up for auction. The intervention of local church leaders and the media at the auction sale resulted in the house being withdrawn from sale, exposure of illegal practices, and a TV investigation that uncovered other victims.

The fraud was exposed. That family was able to keep their house, receive assistance to help them through a tight spot, and recovered quickly to become well-functioning and self-supporting. However, if the worker had not asked deeper questions of the situation the family may well have entered into a downwards spiral of poverty and need.

In our analysis, we may ask questions to help find causes of suffering and injustice

- What are the factors contributing to this injustice? Greed, fear, alienation, apathy, power imbalance and so on.
- Which of these factors are obvious, and which are hidden?
- Why are people behaving unjustly?
- What belief or cultural systems are keeping this injustice in place?
- Are there political or organisational systems contributing to this injustice?
- What is a personal failure here, and what is a system failure?

Engaging the (God) Biblical Perspective

Prophets bring a divine perspective; they hear the voice of God.

> Isaiah: 'for the Lord speaks' (Isaiah 1:2, NASB)
>
> Micah: 'the word of the Lord that came to Micah' (Micah 1:1)
>
> Amos: 'two years before the earthquake the Lord gave me several messages' (Amos 1: 1, CEV)
>
> Joel: 'this is the message the Lord gave to me' (Joel 1:1, CEV)

Any social reformer would consider the context and analyse what is going on, but engaging the sacred story is a point of difference for the prophets (people) of God – those who would act with social justice from within the Christian tradition. Christian social justice cannot stop with simply understanding the context and analysing the underlying political, economic and social systems. Christians are required to engage the God perspective, primarily obtained from studying and understanding the Bible with seriousness. That biblical consideration is further enhanced by prayer, and consideration within a context of worship which has a proper regard for keeping our imaginations alive as God would want them to be. Christian social reformers hear the voice of God, and only then do the required actions become clear.

One of the frequent criticisms of social justice response is that people rush straight into action without analysis or a proper regard for the divine perspective. When Moses tried to deal with the injustice in a rush, it ended badly. He murdered the oppressor and became the oppressed, in one swift, rash moment. When Moses started listening to God a whole new approach to overcoming oppression emerged. He was able to lead a defeat of oppression and his people to freedom in ways he could not have imagined. We are led and guided by God's word. When we consider social and economic injustices alongside the promise and reality of a biblical view, we have the ability to deliver permanent damage to injustice.

Social Action

Prophets inspire, lead and take action. They do something about it. They don't just see, they're not just moved, they don't just weep, they don't just analyse and work out what is wrong, they don't just hear the voice of God in scripture and prayer; they do something. They challenge injustice with just action.

Bramwell Booth was concerned about the age of young girls involved in prostitution. He certainly learned all he could about what and why this was happening. He prayed and preached that the use of girls in prostitution was a breach of God's purpose for their lives. But he did not stop there. He took action to get things to change. He stirred up a national debate about young girls being taken as sex slaves. Then, to prove what was happening, he and William Stead got themselves arrested for procurement. When these actions created a movement for change, Booth started a national petition that eventually got the law amended.

Bramwell Booth experienced the tragedy of what was happening to young girls (understood the context), researched what was going on (analysed the context), prayed and preached (engaged the divine perspective), and then took action (social action).

When faced with injustice, two errors have sometimes characterized the Christian response. Either we have seen, analysed and heard the voice of God to do something and not responded, or we have rushed into action without seeing, analysing and hearing the voice of God.

Another common error is to forget in our analysis that the people and communities actually living within the injustice are best able to defeat it. They are the ones who will help us to understand the depths of the issue, and they have the capacity to help lead the fight. So often we overlook the knowledge and strength that exists within communities by doing our analysis and acting on their behalf without true consultation.

The Christian church has made and still makes all of these errors. As Christians we need to know culture and context, analyse it using the best of tools, introduce to it the sacred story and then involve ourselves in changing the world.

The Catholic Young Christian Workers movement developed a second tool for theological analysis: 'See, Judge, Act'. This model was used to help its members to examine the underlying causes and consequences of social injustice, challenge existing structures on those issues, achieve change in the individual and their environment, and activate others to take action. They developed See, Judge, Act as a way of living out the gospel.

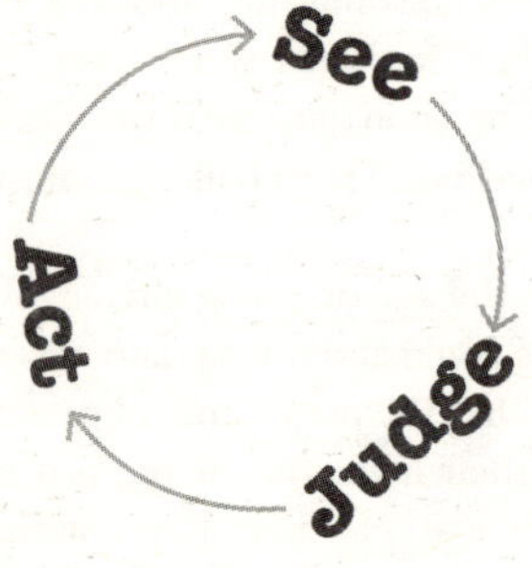

See, Judge, Act

See, Judge, Act is a way of undertaking a social justice ministry either personally or in a group. It represents the simple application of biblical truth to life events in a way that can be hugely effective.

It involves three things:

1. **See.** Recognizing what is happening in a particular situation.
2. **Judge.** Analysing what is going on from a theological, economic and social framework.
3. **Act.** Undertake some action to bring about change.

See

Seeing involves asking a number of questions

- What is actually happening?
- What is this doing to people?

- Why is this happening?
- Who is doing something about this?
- What effect are these actions having?

The first step in any Christian social justice approach requires that we understand, see and feel the situation. We must know the reality at street level. It can't be from a distance, such as from an office somewhere else, removed from the situation. It must be from the 'heat of the battle'. Far too many decisions on social action made by the church today come from offices, boardrooms and places removed from where the real pain is occurring. The concern to act is commendable, but there is an enormous risk involved in taking on social evil when you are distant from the people whose lives are affected by the injustice.

In the theological action/reflection process this street-level engagement is called 'understanding the context'. In this model, the term is 'seeing'. We dare not proceed into action without this understanding, feeling, and experiencing the lives of people impacted by social evil. We need to put ourselves in their shoes.

Jesus said to Zaccheus, 'I am coming to your house for tea.' Why? Because he knew that this identification, this close encounter and personal knowledge was going to build the base for repentance and change. And so it did.

This is an approach to adopt both as individuals and in our communities. The church needs to become a learning organization, linking local action and response with organizational change. The partnership between those in the field and those in policy is crucial if we are going to remain relevant in our ever-changing communities. In other words, policy needs to be consistently informed by field experience.

'A key pathway for developing and maintaining dynamic positive partnership and sustaining learning is the systematic involvement by organizations in learning.'[97]

We need to invite policy makers and leadership to participate in the community environment, invite them into the context – literally, into the homes as Jesus modelled. We need to share space for learning together so they too can empathize and understand the current reality of the injustices. We need to create opportunities for 'mutual sharing of vision, as well as the challenges and struggles faced by both the local team and the leadership.'[98]

The Booth–Tucker Institute in Vancouver was designed for leaders. Part of its intention is to place leaders into the thick of things, among the poorest people in the city. Instead of a retreat centre for escape, the leadership school is created to give an immersion experience to leaders who by the nature of their job, have been distanced from the people they have been called to serve. The decent hotel is gone, and offered in its place is a slum rooming house. In only a week, leaders consistently go from distant advocates for the marginalized to friends of the poor. Experience has shown that their ministry takes on a new vibrancy and their passion is re-ignited for the Kingdom.[99]

The Five Principles

When we are with people in their context, we need to be suspicious and question what we are experiencing because our own enculturation and personal history can send us down the wrong track. McAfee Brown suggests using what he calls the five principles of hermeneutic suspicion when we are doing and 'seeing' the context.[100]

Principle One: What we see is not necessarily what is there

McAfee Brown suggests that seeing contexts as a Christian or with the eyes of God is a particular way of looking at the world. This is reflected through the Old Testament prophets. As you read, it becomes clear that they saw the world in a different way to most. Their view was frequently a minority view and often not shared by those in leading positions.

We should look with the understanding that what we see is not necessarily what is there.

Someone may ask for shelter but as we really get to know them, we may discover that what they actually need is help to get employment, support in challenging an injustice and long-term housing assistance so that they don't pay 70 per cent of their income just maintaining a roof over their heads.

In the words of Rob Bell, 'This is really about that.'[101]

Sometimes other people, local authorities and governments go to some trouble to stop us seeing what is really happening. In the days of apartheid the South African government would often bring visitors to South Africa to show them that black people were happy and living well under the system. The visitors never got to see the places where black misery was rife. Similar things happen regularly at world events like the Olympics, of which Beijing is the latest example: people technically see, but it's a controlled glimpse. Often the unpleasant parts are hidden. In

Vancouver, Canada, the index of a tourist map for the downtown area was placed over the poorest section of the city.

At other times we can live somewhere and not see what is going on in our own backyard, or we justify it with a different interpretation. As recorded in the Bible, Amos saw things others did not see – and so did Jesus.

We can visit a country as a tourist and not understand a great deal about the politics, social health or true wellbeing of people in that country. We have listened to people who have become experts on some place they visited for a week. Would we see all that you see? A tourist does not gain an accurate picture of the political system of a country.

So we need to have a natural suspicion and question of what we see. We need to ask *is this really the truth?*

As a Christian leader I often had someone from Head Office visit the church. On most occasions, what the leader saw was not what was usually happening. People came who we didn't usually see, the musicians practised harder and people helped to make the occasion very special. Of course, there were also those who complained to the leader about things they had never mentioned before. I am sure that most of the leaders were wise enough to know what they were seeing was part of the truth, but not all of it.

Campbell

Principle Two: What we see depends on where we are standing

What we see depends on our own experience, beliefs, friends, social standing and upbringing, just to name a few factors. We are not unbiased when we experience a situation. Our own position and history impact upon our worldview and affect how we interpret different events.

If you asked the question 'How is your country doing?' we predict that an unemployed person, a successful businessman, an indigenous person and the minister of finance would each give you a valid but different view. Their view would be affected by their position, history, training and experience.

> *During my school career I gained one view of the settlement and history of New Zealand. That viewpoint was extremely biased towards a positive presentation of British colonization and European settlement. Later in life, as I started to learn the same history from a Maori viewpoint, I realized that many of the assumptions my attitudes were based on were incorrect, and needed to be rethought in light of my new information from Maori history.*
>
> Campbell

A number of things can affect how we view what is happening: our upbringing, our religion and family, even our politics. How the average American views the success of the Iraq war will be influenced by whether they are Republican or Democrat.

Principle Three: When others tell us what they see, we need to know where they are standing as well as where we are standing

> *In my current appointment, I frequently meet with people who are extremely wealthy. They often give me their views on welfare, heath care, education and other social issues. In weighing up what they say, it is really important for me to know a little about them and to consider where they are coming from in relation to me. What is their belief structure? Have they any friends who are poor? How do they feel about the gospel? How much do they gain or lose through what they are saying? What vested interests do they have?*
>
> Campbell

The Christian church needs to consistently question whose voices have the most effect on what we do. Is it the poor we work with, those who are addicted, the indigenous or immigrant women who are numerous in our community services, or our donors, politicians and those who offer us public relations, marketing services or advisory committees? The way Jesus lived suggests we should be most influenced by the voice of the poor. Questioning who we listen to enables some sifting and evaluation of opinions, which are invariably biased according to their viewpoint.

Sometimes our ministries are flawed because we have not updated our understanding of what is happening to people, or our perspective is disconnected. If where we are located determines our viewpoint, then our response to the biblical injunction to side with the poor will be highly significant in choosing where we live, where we work and what organizations we give our time to.

Principle Four: No matter how much anybody sees, nobody sees it all

This means that we must examine a variety of observations, information sources and data in order to arrive at the truth. In some ways this has become easier with the Internet; and in other ways it is more difficult. There is more information and easier access to different views on an issue than ever before, but then, with so many different voices, it is hard to discern which ones we should listen to.

We need to have contestable advice and a variety of sources that we can explore. It is not sensible to rely on just one source for our view of what is going on. We also need to be constantly testing past sources of information to see if they are still reliable.

Principle Five: What we see is always subject to correction

If our viewpoint is always going to be biased, we can never make claims to fully possess absolute truth. This does not deny the concept of absolute truth. It simply negates any individual human's possession of it. We always need to be ready to correct our view.

Having regard for McAfee Brown's principles, how then do we gain information on a social injustice that enables clarity of the issue? One of the answers is to have a variety of sources of information. There are two important questions to ask in order to gain reliable information. What material may be useful and where can it be accessed? Then we need to ask what will be helpful in understanding the context of this situation.

What material may be useful? Some possibilities are:

- Actual stories of what is happening
- Facts on the situation
- Statistics
- Reports and research studies
- Photos and videos

Where can this information be accessed? Some possibilities are:

- National statistic sites (Internet)
- Library
- Archives
- Community centres
- Community surveys (stories of people)

When we have collected the data we need to ask some further questions to understand the context of our information.

- What is its level of reliability?
- What information is missing?
- What does it tell us?
- What are the actions needed?
- What further information do we need?
- What are the macro issues affecting this issue? Economics, social/political pressures, history, past injustice, environment and so on.
- How do they impact our work?
- Do they make a difference to what we do?
- Do they add new information?
- Who are the organizations and groups who might be helpful in working with this problem?
- Who else is effectively doing something about this problem?

By engaging in this thorough examination, we will start to see what is occurring in the issue that concerns us and we are ready to start the process of judging.

Judge
Judging is analysing and asking ourselves some key questions from our Christian tradition.

- What do I think about this as a Christian?
- What does the Bible say?
- Are there gospel narratives and themes that might be relevant?

- What are some relevant teachings of Jesus?
- What are the themes of scripture that apply?
- What does the Holy Spirit reveal to me as I pray about this?
- What are the relevant teaching and experience of the Christian church?
- Are there any lessons that apply from the social teaching of the church?
- Faced with this situation, how have Christian communities acted in the past?

Judging does not involve the application of a few texts to situations of injustice. It requires an understanding of the treatment of injustice in the historical context of scripture and then the testing out and meaning of those truths where contemporary injustice impacts people's lives.

After we have applied biblical truth to a situation, it is time to act.

Act

In thinking about acting for social justice there are some important questions to ask.

What exactly is it that you want to change (long-term goal)?

Do you see something that can be permanently altered?

If you want to change the situation of people currently homeless, are you happy to provide housing for the people you know, or do you want to permanently change the housing policy of the country so that everyone has the right and access to adequate housing?

It is necessary to ask *what actions are needed now* (short-term goal)? On the way to changing the national housing policy, you may want to try to provide immediate temporary accommodation for some people who are homeless.

Having decided on what we want to do, we then need to decide what methods will be most effective. Staying with the problem of homelessness, a number of methods would be possible. An advocacy response that helps people access existing housing, a political response that puts pressure on government for the provision of public housing, a practical response that partners with private or public funding to actually build and supply housing, or a policy response that develops research and reports that help to change national housing policy and start a program to eradicate homelessness. Most problems usually require a mixture of methods dealing with various aspects of the problem.

Having identified the method, it is important to identify *what spiritual resources are necessary to undertake this action?* Prophetic action can be an uphill struggle. You can be misunderstood and you can often be working against the status quo wisdom. The result can be tiredness, hurt feelings, some confrontation and a sense of isolation in the struggle for justice. If a Christian is to survive these pressures, it is vital they think through a way of being spiritually resourced.

Then decide *who can be involved in this action?* Who are the allies, what skills are needed, how will the team be formed to ensure success? In a struggle to defeat homelessness we would need many skills – including practical, advocacy and research skills. Finally, do not forget to celebrate and include the injustice you are acting upon in the context of worship. Worship is the place where our imagination of what God's world is like is fired up; it should be a place of social justice empowerment and a place where we celebrate the triumph of justice over evil and injustice.

Summary

Both the 'Biblical Action Reflection' and the 'See, Judge, Act' methodologies have three major components in the work of Christian social justice.

They require that we:

1. Confront the injustice, having regard for the context and cause of the injustice.
2. Ask questions of the injustice in light of scripture, Christian thought, history and prayer.
3. Take some action, evaluating its result and celebrating what is achieved.

Prayer

May I have ears to hear what the Lord is saying and
eyes to see what the Lord is doing,
May I have a mind to learn what the Lord is teaching,
and a heart to love the Lord and my neighbour as myself.
Amen.

EIGHT: POLITICAL RESPONSE

Just imagine a world where politics delivers just systems not riddled with corruption and bribery. Political systems that deliver to every child in the world adequate levels of food, education and health care. Politicians that don't rely on war, terrorism and weapons of massive destruction to settle difference and allocate land and oil. World political systems that allow mothers to go to bed at night knowing their children are safe and that they can have a future free of need, injustice and discrimination. Imagine such a world.

In recent times within the church, members who have made statements, or challenged an action of the government or a political party have often been criticized. Politics, particularly when it means aligning with one side of the political divide, is seen to be messy and risky. There is a fear that to criticize the government means we will threaten our funding, or that we'll lose their respect and our reputation. The reality is that most governments, although they may be angry or annoyed at the criticism, are unlikely to respond by withdrawing funding if the criticism is well-founded and robust.[102] But regardless of whether they do or don't, the guiding principles for people of the gospel must always be to stand and speak for truth no matter what the cost. After all, the one we follow was crucified because he spoke out about the abuses of power and the oppressive practices of the ecclesiastical leadership and politicians.

To engage in political activity is also difficult because within any population there are also a variety of views that can be held.

In considering political action as part of a social justice ministry, two major issues arise. Firstly, what is the legitimate role of politics in the life and ministry of a Christian; and secondly, how do we use political action within our own denominations to challenge injustice?

Although we should be suspicious of an approach to social justice ministry that sees involvement in politics as the *only* way to tackle injustice in the world, we must acknowledge that politics has an important and legitimate role in a Christian ministry of social justice.

Some important theological principles lie at the heart of political action:

- The Bible does not differentiate between the spiritual and the secular, the personal and the public, the evangelical and the political.
- God is biased towards the poor and expects his disciples to change political and government systems if they stand in the way of justice.
- The prophetic role of the faith community is both to denounce those things inconsistent with gospel truth and to announce the Good News.
- Any response to sin and evil involves the challenging of evil at both a personal and structural level.

Politics often takes on a false mystique, but at its heart it has to do with the organization of human affairs. It describes the regulation, ordering and ideological underpinning of human society. As such, politics is an almost universal concept, encompassing a wide spectrum of life and experience. The idea that certain areas of life such as sport or religion are free from politics must be resisted. These activities are political both internally and in relation to society at large.

For instance, in considering the way sport is structured internationally, issues like power, rules and money are all political issues. In society, sport will play a function in the lives of citizens, and therefore be regulated and perhaps even sponsored by a central government. At times (the 2008 Beijing Olympics for starters!)[103] sport or an aspect of it may become a major political issue, affecting the lives of those who would normally have no contact with it.

There is no option for Christians to exist in a non-political way. People who do not vote, or who withdraw from involvement in political issues, are in fact simply lending support to the status quo. As the industrial society becomes more complex, technology has enabled greater centralization and a global consciousness has emerged. Political issues have become ever more pervasive and universal.

Langdon Gilkey writes in *Reaping the Whirlwind* that we experience history as either a stream of possibility in which we have freedom and influence, or as a capricious tide of events by which we are trapped and over which we have no control. Gilkey characterized these two ways of experiencing life as destiny and fate respectively. The task of politics is to turn fate into destiny; to enable us to gain a sense of control over history.

This, however, is a fundamentally religious question. If we believe that God is working in human history for his purpose, and that he is sovereign, then the fundamental question of all concrete political life is a faith question. If God is involved in the shaping of history – and this is the testimony of scripture – then politics will always be a religious issue. In the film *Amazing Grace*, Wilberforce debates whether he should serve God or his country, until an abolitionist suggests that if he pushes to end slavery, he can do both.

In the political realm of social justice, sometimes the gospel may be in harmony with the policies and actions of a government or political movement, while at other times the actions of politicians and governments may contradict a gospel understanding.

As Christians, it is important that we do not choose neutrality from politics as the safe and comfortable option. Saying nothing or remaining neutral is in fact supporting the current political climate. While it is true that the primary purpose of the church is not politics but rather the creation of a just society, this vision has political consequences.

Pastor Martin Niemöller wrote:

'In Germany, they came first for the Communists,

And I didn't speak up because I wasn't a Communist;

And then they came for the trade unionists,

And I didn't speak up because I wasn't a trade unionist;

And then they came for the Jews,

And I didn't speak up because I wasn't a Jew;

And then . . . they came for me . . .

And by that time there was no one left to speak up.'[104]

The Role of Politics in the Church

So should Christians be involved in politics? It has already been demonstrated from the biblical tradition that certain elements of faith call for a response that is political. The concern for justice – the protection of vulnerable groups within society – and the call for social responsibility from those in power are issues that can only be fully addressed in contemporary society through political involvement.

Following Jesus through active discipleship requires a re-ordering of priorities, a change of lifestyle, the breaking of castes, conflict with authorities, and the announcing of a Kingdom that will bring to an end all temporal powers. The choice for the Christian church is therefore not between involvement in politics or non-involvement, but between biblical faith and non-biblical faith.

Why then is there the widespread perception today that the Christian church sits on the sidelines and sees political involvement as a distraction from its main business? Some of the possibilities are:

1. *The presence of a false spirituality militates against social or political involvement*

   It makes spirituality a private inner experience with no connection to the outside world. This is a spirituality that says it is possible to love God without loving your neighbour.

4. *A desire to protect the church*

   A major reason for political non-involvement is the institutional structure of the church. In order to survive over time, denominations have adopted strong institutional forms. As politics is about power and inevitably involves conflict, the Christian church has retreated from conflict with governments and politicians as a means of self-preservation. It has also avoided becoming unduly concerned in situations where political involvement may threaten the funding sources.

5. *A reluctance to accept a contemporary call to the cross*

   Recovery of the wider dimensions of the gospel in the modern world results in confrontation with the world, and often inevitably, the cross.

6. *A misunderstanding of political alignment*

   The Christian church is not uninvolved in politics, but is often a bastion of conservative political thought. That is, through its life and teaching, it promotes the conservation of the way things are. It therefore unwittingly lends support to injustice.[105]

6. *A desire to manage the risk*

   It is a legitimate activity to want to protect the church by managing risk. Risk, however, is part and parcel of the gospel and we need to be willing to take risks. One of the greatest assets the Christian church has is the high public regard in which it is held. Sometimes this regard may need to be risked on behalf of the poor. For example, one church decided to support the families and children of rubbish collectors who had been on strike for weeks by providing them with food. Members of the public who had not had their rubbish collected for six weeks were incensed that the church action might prolong the strike.

> The church's decision was made as a response to the gospel; some donors were lost but the integrity and commitment of the church to the gospel it preached was preserved.

Social justice requires a conversion from these approaches and a commitment to be involved in all the affairs of men and women, whether personal, social or political, so that the Christian church can be the church of the poor. The mission of Christ means, as it always has done, an involvement.

Possible Political Approaches

It would be helpful to consider some of the different political approaches used in history. These fall into the following categories:

1. *Party Politics Option*

   Christians can become active members of existing political parties or stand for political office. This approach takes the political situation seriously and argues that if Christian ideals are to be attained within history, it will only be through participation in the existing political processes. Christians who gain political power are able to have direct influence on real issues. Those active in party membership are 'salt' within the organization. They do not retreat from the difficult issues or ambiguity of the real world. On the negative side, the party system is such that one is bound to the confines of party loyalty, which often calls for compromise and even contradiction of faith-convictions.

2. *The Revolutionary Options*

   Revolutions are another form of direct political involvement. The revolutionary option allows involvement with political change without (at least initially) the compromise associated with party politics. Revolutions often result from a sustained identification with the poor and victims of an unjust society. To take the revolutionary option is to be convinced of the rightness of one's own position and to 'push' history in a certain direction. This involves a large degree of presumption. It is helpful to remember that the Christian state of America was established through revolution, and that respected theologians such as Dietrich Bonhoeffer have been involved in revolutionary activity.

3. *The Alternative Option*

   Some Christians argue that the responsibility of Christians is to model a different way of living based on the Kingdom of God; to provide the world with an alternative model of human existence. Though not directly involved in politics, such a community will have political significance because it stands as a challenge to the existing order. Jesus did not directly participate in political life, yet by positioning himself with the marginalized he had a great deal of political impact. The church is to challenge the status quo through its very life and existence.

   This is an enormously attractive approach in that it allows Christians to maintain ethical purity and avoid compromise. It picks up on the biblical theme of light, and operates through persuasion rather than employing the more brutal tools of power politics.

4. *Standing with the Poor Option*

   Often, those who respond to the poor by working with them become aware of the social and political causes of such poverty. To simply meet the immediate needs of a disadvantaged group is not enough as it may help to maintain the situation of injustice that has disadvantaged them in the first place. A more effective response normally requires intervention on the political level. Christians working with the poor and involved in social service can do this effectively from the base of established credibility, as people more informed and in touch with the reality of the situation. Political action often grows out of a ministry situation and responds to the concrete issues involved. It allows for long-term strategies, local knowledge, and easy evaluation of developments. The ministry of Martin Luther King, Jr. is a good example of an issue-related political response, which grew out of working alongside an oppressed people. King demonstrated how traditional Christian symbols like public prayer and preaching could become instruments of social and political change.

In a situation of injustice, it is sometimes a political action even to serve the poor, because this brings attention to the unpleasant facts that governments would prefer remained hidden. There is a certain inevitability about the conflict that arises when Christians choose to side with the poor rather than the powerful.

This approach to political involvement is not tied to a particular political analysis or ideology, but grows instead from an active discipleship.

Christians are able to maintain Christian authenticity by acting in a way consistent with faith. It has the added benefit of dealing with political issues as they affect real people, rather than in the abstract.

Social justice engagement with politics requires a consideration of which of these options offers the most viable approach for action and then a decision about the method for involvement.

Workable Methods in Political Action

The methods that can be used to involve politics in social justice action are many and varied and need to be appropriate to the cause or issue being addressed. Since its early history, one of the methods the church has used is that of protest. Protesting the right to use the street for meetings and protesting the age of consent to the English Parliament through petition are some early examples. It seems, however, that protesting is no longer a welcome methodology in the modern church. In places where we have become highly respected institutions in the community – the upholders of values of decency and correctness – using protest doesn't seem to fit. But there is still a place for protest. Sometimes the issues are so monumental and the resistance to change so strong, that the only political statement that can be made for justice is to protest on the street or in a public place.

For example, when a rent freezer was not working in a community, the simple but effective placement of an old broken freezer with a sign proclaiming 'The rent freezer is not working' in the foyer of the Government Housing Corporation created national media interest and stimulated a public debate that resulted in a change of policy and approach to rent assistance. Protest is often a way of giving power to the victims; they can become engaged and help to achieve change for themselves.

Often political action can be triggered by research documents that provide alternatives in an area of injustice. *In Darkest England and the Way Out* provided a model and detailed plan of how life could be different for England's submerged tenth. William Booth used the Darkest England plan on a world tour to engage politicians and people of influence. A well-researched and argued report on a local issue can often be a helpful instrument for change. Research of this type needs to use sound and trustworthy methodologies and be well-presented and distributed, with good follow-up.

The Christian church often uses the media to advertise and inform people of its work and appeal for public financial support. But the media is also a key weapon in bringing about political change. To motivate politicians to act often requires education that will change public opinion towards the solutions being argued for. When sensitively and strategically used, the media can be a powerful tool for social justice action.

Often a most effective way of bringing about social change as we challenge injustice is by becoming part of the political process. Christians committed to social justice are needed at a political and official level in local and national government. Christians must encourage and support these people as they work for public office. Ways of assisting them include providing training, helping with the election process, supporting and mentoring[106] when these individuals are elected, and surrounding them with prayer and support.

In addition to direct political involvement, we should recognize that important decisions and policy changes are undertaken by working parties, commissions and other government consultative mechanisms. The Christian church should always have lists of Christians committed to social justice categorized in various areas of activity. As vacancies are advertised for these groups, these individuals should be offered for membership and involvement. Believers who are offered the opportunity to contribute to government committees and working parties should be supported and encouraged by the church. Additionally, there are always opportunities to partner with other organizations and campaigns in social justice projects.

Meeting with local and national politicians can provide useful opportunities to present documentation and argument for social change. Social justice action requires us to identify people who can influence change – they too need to build relationships that will enable them to receive reports and information on situations of social injustice that need attention. Regular reporting by one group on poverty in their area triggered a mayoral task force on poverty and the initiation of community support.

If social justice is to happen, we must engage politically. Climate change, poverty, HIV and AIDS, sexual trafficking, unjust trade practices, and homelessness are just some of the areas in which politics must be engaged if real change is to occur.

The methods of political involvement are not fixed. There are tried and proven ways but the answer in a particular situation may be something innovative and new. This is a ministry for imagination and divine creativity.

During his two years as Bishop of Santiago de Maria, Oscar Romero criss-crossed his diocese on horseback, talking with labouring families to learn how he could best serve them. The reality of their lives horrified the bishop. Every day he discovered children dying because their parents could not pay for simple penicillin; people who were paid less than half of the legal minimum wage; people who had been savagely beaten for 'insolence' after they asked for long overdue pay. Romero began using the resources of the diocese – and his own personal resources – to help the poor, but he knew that simple charity was not enough. He wrote in his diary:

'The world of the poor teaches us that liberation will arrive only when the poor are not simply on the receiving end of handouts from government or from churches, but when they themselves are the masters and protagonists of their own struggle for liberation.'

Similarly, in a pastoral letter released in November 1976, he reflected on the plight of the thousands of coffee plantation workers in his diocese:

'The Church must cry out by command of God: "God has meant the earth and all it contains for the use of the whole human race. Created wealth should reach all in just form, under the aegis of justice and accompanied by charity . . ." It saddens and concerns us to see the selfishness with which means and dispositions are found to nullify the just wage of the harvesters. How we would wish that the joy of this rain of rubies and all the harvests of the earth would not be darkened by the tragic sentence of the Bible: "Behold, the day wage of labourers that cut your fields defrauded by you is crying out, and the cries of the reapers have reached the ears of the Lord"' (James 5:4).[107]

Prayer

May the God who gives endurance and encouragement give you a spirit of unity among yourselves as you follow Christ Jesus, so that with one heart and mouth you may glorify the God and Father of our Lord Jesus Christ. (Romans 15:5-6)

Just imagine a world where every Christian and the church as a whole are passionate to live justly. Where Christians toss and turn at night because children die due to a lack of clean water, or because other children step on landmines while they play; a world where the church is restless to do something about poverty, racism, malnutrition and environmental destruction; a world where Christians all have friends who are poor, friends of another skin colour and ethnicity, and friends whose hope has been extinguished. A church where our commitment to God is measured not by how many love songs to Jesus we can sing in an hour, but by our actions to bring justice, mercy and faith to other people. Imagine such a world.

NINE: PRACTICAL RESPONSE

Taking practical action is the risky part – because there is no prescription, no 'magic solution' to stop injustice, no marked-out route to get there. Instead there is a response and an invitation to journey towards justice which we can all walk together. The problem is that we want to get there in ten easy steps. But humans are complex and, more often than not, the journey is cyclical – we take a step forward and need to re-assess, learn, and take another step. There are a million steps to be taken, all of them equally important and requiring unity in the body of Christ. But as Gary Haugen, founder of the International Justice Mission, pointed out in *Terrify No More*, often the hardest part of social justice is simply getting started.

To move forward you need to struggle through many issues, both inside and out. Inside, we battle against depression, cynicism, fear and guilt. Outside, we face apathy, indifference, defiance and greed. Both foes are formidable, but we suggest that, like David facing Goliath, if we throw our lives on God then we'll emerge with the right strategy to bring down the giants of injustice.

Practical responses to injustice need to occur at a number of levels.

This means that both individually and corporately efforts to tackle social injustice must occur on all levels. These areas are not mutually exclusive and, in our shrinking world, a particular injustice may need to be tackled at each level through a connected and expanding effort.

Individual Response

The first level consists of *individuals* deciding to do something about injustice in the world. This is probably the simplest yet most challenging path for us to travel. It is about consistently choosing the way of justice in the face of temptation and trial.

Individual social justice action is often more about the way we live than what we do. In the words of Walter Brueggemann, 'Social action ministry does not consist of spectacular acts of social crusading or of abrasive measures of indignation. Rather it is offering in the everyday an alternative perception of reality and in letting people see their own history in the light of God's will for justice. Not in the big issues of the day but wherever people try to live together and worry about their future and their identity.'[108]

Action generally doesn't occur until we begin to feel and understand the injustice people suffer in their lives. We are then only sustained in that journey as Christian disciples when biblical justice starts to take personal root and shape how we live and act.

To start to live and act justly we propose:

- Actively paying attention to the theology of justice in the Bible.
- Shaping worship and prayers to help us imagine God's ideal of freedom and justice for all people.
- Asking ourselves how we can change aspects of our daily living to lessen the pain or injustice others are suffering, or avoid creating more injustice in the world.
- Starting to take small steps to tackle injustice.

This means that, depending on where we are starting, our practical responses will be different. For some it may mean taking the uncomfortable step of placing themselves in proximity with the poor. For others, it is a commitment to live simply.[109] The responses are endless. Just imagine.

Individual practical responses could be:

- Increase your tithing/offerings.[110]
- Volunteer at a local organization – help out at a soup kitchen, tutor new migrants, befriend youth 'at risk'.
- Share your home with an asylum seeker.
- Practice hospitality.
- Practice generosity.
- Support an advocacy campaign, read up and get informed.
- Sponsor a child or community.
- Shop at charity shops and say no to the excessive demands for 'new things'.
- Have a 'Buy Nothing Day'[111] once a week.
- Go Fairtrade.
- Choose to live locally and support local small businesses.
- Find ways to drive less.
- Become aware of injustices behind your consumer choices, such as labour abuses in sweatshops.
- Move into an incarnational community.[112]

Tony Campolo and Gordon Aeschliman provide a huge list of individual and local action in their book *Everybody Wants to Change the World*, and *Breaking With Business as Usual: Achieving the Millennium Development Goals* by Caritas Internationalis also suggests a range of ideas to get involved. Check them out.

While no individual can address every issue of injustice, the world would be dramatically different if every Christian took an area of social injustice in their community and imagined it differently. Imagine everyone acting to confront and defeat injustice. Christians can support the rights of Maori and Aboriginals, they can stand alongside asylum seekers and refugees, they can make direct efforts to communicate with those who are alone, homeless, addicted or whose minority status means they are unsupported. The actions of Christians should make sure that the people society discards and marginalizes know and feel they are beloved children of God.

Living justly starts alternative ways of existing that support those who suffer injustice and deprivation and these spread to others. One person deciding to look into the issues surrounding trade and consumer choices can stimulate others to buy Fairtrade products.

Community Response

Just as God created us to live in community, he calls us to seek justice together. There is no doubt that as you start to engage with issues you will want to seek out others who are also passionate about social justice, in order to join with them in a mutual commitment to make a difference.

This may mean joining a group, linking to an organization working for social justice or participation in a campaign to bring social or economic change. Groups can often make a far greater impact than an individual. Groups provide a place for support in the journey toward justice. What starts as an individual commitment develops into a collective commitment, in which each of us plays an important role.

In the UK and across Europe there are many local organizations tackling an area of injustice. Support them, join them.

Similarly, a Christian community should always make sure there is a mechanism ready to support people in the congregation as they work out their social justice passions. Communities need to offer every encouragement and spiritual nourishment.

Worship should be constructed regularly to provide a vision of how the world should be when justice reigns. It can continually challenge people to live counter-culturally, confronting consumerism and environmental destruction and call us to be a people living for justice.

A possible mechanism to foster and encourage social justice action is the formation of social justice clusters. Social justice clusters are small groups that come together for social action. They can provide the opportunity for discussion about the biblical and theological aspects of acting for social justice. The prophetic See, Judge, Act methods can be used by the group. They can be places where people pray through areas of injustice and encourage the development of an action plan. Providing the opportunity to develop and support living justly is an essential part of dynamic discipleship. Working for social justice can create opposition or misunderstanding and a cluster provides the place for pastoral support and reflection on the appropriateness of actions undertaken.

Practical responses in community

- Community gardens/kitchens.
- Relational tithe.[113]
- Common purse.
- Community dinners.
- Lobby local councils, governments – raise awareness about issues facing the community.
- Sponsor a community as a community.[114]
- Host community discussion groups to stimulate action on issues in the local community.

National and International Responses

Sometimes certain injustices are so widespread that the causes and impact goes beyond the local and require a national or international response. Amnesty International,[115] Stop The Traffik[116] and Greenpeace[117] are examples of human justice and environmental justice campaigns that have moved across national borders to become international campaigns.

At these levels we often feel powerless to change the situation. However, it is important that as individuals, local communities and national organizations we continue to voice our discontent with the situation, calling for justice and change from the places of power.

National organizations often provide coordinated vehicles for action against larger social injustices. In the UK there are national organizations working to alleviate poverty, protect the environment, advocating for prison reform, preventing human trafficking, assisting refugees and supporting AIDS victims. Churches and communities can form helpful partnerships with these organizations in their efforts to undertake a social justice ministry.

National and international practical responses:

- Get involved and support national and international campaigns.
- Lobby your government to fulfil their promise on the 0.7 per cent Official Development Assistance Goal.[118]
- Engage in advocacy/political intervention for the poor.
- Use the power of the Christian church for social justice issues, not just for fundraising or evangelism.
- Train and equip people for lives of justice.
- Build strong international partnerships between denominations.
- Create outlets for products made overseas.

How and where to start?

1. *Keep looking, asking, questioning, and thinking.*

   One of the great temptations in this generation is to 'shut off'. We don't want to think or probe because it ends up making us feel uncomfortable. But that is exactly where we need to be in order to create change. It's not an easy option, but we encourage you to be wide-eyed in your living and watching.

2. *Get closer to the people who suffer from the injustice.*

   Proximity is an important key to the solution. Become a 'learner' of the poor. Shane Claiborne explains, 'It is a beautiful thing when folks in poverty are no longer just a missions project but become genuine friends and family with whom we laugh, cry, dream, and struggle . . . that's when things get messy. When people begin moving beyond charity and toward justice and solidarity with the poor and oppressed, as Jesus did, they get in trouble. Once we are actually friends with folks in the struggle, we start to ask why people are poor, which is never as popular as giving charity.'[119]

My friend Elizabeth told me about a friend from the developing world finding her on Facebook. Excited to have made the connection, she also shared how conscious she became of her lifestyle – asking herself what her Facebook profile page and photos looked like from a developing world perspective. The fear of transparency is a natural one. There was a clear tension in feeling superficial and rich in light of the life her friend came from.

Danielle

3. *Identify an injustice and become informed about it.*

   Remember that in today's world ignorance is a choice. Be intentional about awareness.

4. *Use the prophetic and systemic tools to uncover the roots of the injustice.*

   This will protect you from shallow responses that end in discouragement and will enable you to produce strategies that will be long-term and bear fruit. The process may take longer, yet the results will be worth it.

5. *Accountability.*

   We use accountability a lot in personal situations: exercise, diet, and finances. Why not justice? Since justice is about relationships, it makes sense that we create accountability structures around and through our justice journey.

The following guide is one way of structuring that accountability.

Just: Tri

We've already offered a systemic model for breaking down large-scale injustices. The journey towards justice also needs to be broken down into smaller steps because endurance is crucial for a long trip. The accountability system we want to suggest now is in keeping with the previous three-part model and offers a way of incorporating justice into our everyday lives. Offered here is a brief explanation of some accountability questions to use in a group.

Personal Circle: Jesus focused

A personal connection with God is central to social justice. Mother Teresa thought her nuns were scraping by on only two hours of personal prayer and meditation everyday. John Wesley felt four was adequate. In *Be A Hero*, Court and Campbell suggest that 'praying the Bible' is the first step to becoming a hero. 'Prayer glorifies God, disciples our own hearts, and brings his will on earth. Prayer is the beginning of the first commandment and it will inevitable lead you to the second."[120]

Certainly anyone who connects with God in the Bible will start to share his heart for the poor.

Our personal connection and relationship with God is made alive in Jesus. He redeems us and is saving us daily. Paul prays, 'May God Himself, the God of peace, sanctify you through and through. May your whole spirit, soul and body be kept blameless at the coming of our Lord Jesus Christ. The one who calls you is faithful and he will do it.' (1 Thessalonians 5:23-24). We are not alone on this journey. Injustice can lead to despair if we don't allow God to show us the final picture. Keeping ourselves alive and spiritually healthy is an important part of the journey.

The three parts of our Personal Circle

- Spirit: our God connection.
  (prayer life, Bible study, God's presence.)
- Soul: mind, will, emotions.
- Body: shape, weight, health.

Questions for accountability in the Personal Circle

- Is my spirit connecting to God? How?
- Are my mind, will and emotions submitted to God's will?
- Am I hearing His voice?
- Am I reading His word?
- Do I honour God with my body?

Community Circle: God the Father focused

Somehow, in the midst of a rugged individualistic society, we have made our faith personal. We've made it a 'quiet time' between God and ourselves where 'our' relationship with God is no one else's business. This has not only destroyed the essence of Christian community but has damaged Christianity itself. Our faith was never intended to be about 'me and God'. There is no 'individual' focus in the Word of God. Our faith only makes sense in community. It is worked out in love through relationships.

The breakdown of community has had a tragic effect on the world, and it is due in part to the erosion of Christian community. We are the salt of the earth. Our ability to relate to people around us with love and compassion is what offers hope and meaning to life. Without this presence in the world, Christ is unrepresented, and hope is lost.

To restore the priority of community we can hold each other accountable to these areas.

The three sections of our community circle

- Faith: how our faith is working out in community/ true humility.
- Mercy: how we express God's compassion through mercy in our communities.
- Justice: how we engage with God's heart for justice.

Questions for accountability in the community circle

- Am I actively involved in Christian community?
- Do I share my life with others?
- Am I merciful? Does mercy flow through me? How?
- What kind of justice is on my heart? How am I actively pursuing justice right now?

World Circle: Holy Spirit focused

Jesus began his ministry with a declaration, 'The Spirit of the Lord is on me, because he has anointed me' (Luke 4:18). When he had completed his mission and was headed heavenward, Jesus instructed his disciples to wait for the Spirit to come upon them with power, 'and you will be my witnesses in Jerusalem, and in all Judea and Samaria, and to the ends of the earth.' (Acts 1:8) This Kingdom is an ever-expanding one. Those who believe in King Jesus will soon catch the vision that his gospel is for the whole world. God is not limited by colour, language, size or place of origin. He paints a picture of a multitude in heaven from 'every tribe and tongue' that is praising God together. His influence is continually expansive. Love expands.

Relating to the glocal reality of justice, this circle challenges us to be present for Christ where we live – in our Jerusalem. All acts of love are done in small ways and small things. Sometimes it will be to show grace to your own spouse or child, sometimes to your colleagues at work. It will also relate to your Samaria, or the places that are 'off limits' in normal everyday life. Samaria was a place that the disciples wouldn't choose to go. It was 'dirty' and considered less valuable to a Jew. God was being specific about his call to the church to take the Spirit to the last, the lost and the least. Finally, this good news is for the whole world. God's plan may have started with a little baby, but it ends with the whole world redeemed. His gospel is global 'good news' and should always be celebrated as that.

The three sections of our World Circle

- Jerusalem: our current circles of influence/family/home church.
- Samaria: the places on the margins/outside the religious camp.
- World: beyond our scope/global vision and impact.

Questions for accountability in the World Circle

- Am I a representative of Jesus at home?
- Do I love my family? How?
- Am I intentional about making relationships with people who aren't like me?
- Have I been 'outside' the religious camp recently?
- Am I aware of the world's needs?

In *Breaking With Business as Usual: Achieving the Millennium Development Goals*, Caritas Internationalis give some great suggestions to help you get started.

Become involved

- by acquiring information and training for community organizing and consciousness raising about the moral issues relating to the MDGs;
- by making personal or local commitments that support the global initiatives of the MDGs, e.g. low energy consumption, recycling, care of natural resources, freedom with regard to consumerism, solidarity-based economics;
- by developing ongoing theological development and JPIC (Justice, Peace, and the Integrity of Creation) educational pro-grammes for parishes, schools, reflection groups, candidates for the consecrated life and the priesthood, and for leaders of Christian communities;
- by tracking and making public the work of the next World Summit which will take place in Rome in May 2007, and whose purpose is to assess the progress made with regard to the Millennium Development Goals.

Participate

- in local and international projects aimed at achieving the eradication of poverty;
- in meetings of human rights groups, social forums, solidarity committees, awareness raising campaigns, and demonstrations against poverty;
- in ecumenical and inter-faith celebrations and prayer services for justice, peace, conversion, and solidarity.

Support and promote

- initiatives that help to eradicate poverty;
- processes that encourage participation, gender equality, open communication, and mutual collaboration;
- 'grassroot groups' that hope to achieve social improvements, especially in the fields of education and healthcare.

Help

- to raise awareness among Roman Catholics that the MDGs and the Catholic Social Teaching are closely related and are an essential part of the Gospel;
- to promote distributive justice so that the 'first world' shares its resources with the poorest countries rather than robbing them;
- to support the voluntary services and development projects of NGOs by offering your time, skills and/or money.

Connect

- with other groups to create solidarity networks that will collaborate for a common cause;
- establish links with civil institutions for any assistance and social promotion they can provide.

Denounce

- oppressive ideologies;
- global imbalances;
- corruption of governments, institutions and organizations.

Lobby and Advocate for

- the respect of human rights;
- the accountability of governments for their promises and actions;
- the achievement of the MDGs in your country by contacting appropriate government officials.

Prayer

I pray God will transform you through inevitable moments of disunity,
I pray you will experience, without doubt,
God's faithfulness and presence in your journey
And I pray that those with whom you meet will see in you a unity of spirit and action, a harmony of word and life,
Because it is in this unity that others will find Jesus.

CONCLUSION: LIVE THE DREAM

Imagine that it wasn't just Nelson Mandela, Desmond Tutu, Martin Luther King, Jr., William Booth, Mother Teresa and Bono who created a better world. **Imagine it was you.** *Imagine that from this moment your life is passionately committed to living a life that would help create the world as God wants it. Imagine what that means for you and the world.*

How do you conclude a book on social justice? By definition, social justice is a new way of seeing the world and a commitment to join the fight against injustice and usher in the Kingdom rule of Christ.

There was a time when extreme poverty was something everyone assumed was going to be around forever. You may have even heard the ideology that we can never eradicate poverty. The mantra is 'Jesus said the poor will be with you always'. But Jesus' commitment to alleviate suffering and his instructions for believers to do the same leads us to believe that his statement is more a call to fight poverty than simply accept it. During the first glimpse of widespread famines, people equated social justice issues with depressing views of the world. Times have changed.

You've now heard world-shapers – in history and in the present – who are singing a new tune. Able to imagine a different world, more and more people are nailing their colours to the mast, ready to join the fight. They are armed with the belief that good is more powerful than evil, that darkness can never extinguish the light and that there is living hope of a new world. We are seeing Jesus' words fulfilled when he spoke to his disciples, 'With man this is impossible, but not with God; all things are possible with God.' (Mark 10:27) This fight takes form in a myriad of colourful campaigns for justice. We celebrate in the diversity of approaches.

Spring Harvest

Every year at Spring Harvest God continues to expand His Kingdom by capturing the imaginations of His people as they gather together, because they believe that the Christian faith is not only about words, it's also about taking action. Over the years, people from Spring Harvest have been instrumental in giving hope to thousands of less fortunate people around the world. Through the offerings project they seek to inform and challenge young people about the issues that cause world need, and show them how, by getting involved, they can make a difference to the lives of others.[121]

At the tenth Spring Harvest in 1988, the attendance topped the 50,000 mark. A popular worship album was launched, with profits going to Christian projects involved in supporting those with AIDS/HIV. It went on to raise over £20,000. Carrying on the tradition of generosity and justice in 1991, £250,000 was given in voluntary offerings for a wide range of Christian work. £49,000 raised for a 'Greener Burkina' by the youth programme was used to replant a forest and build a dam to alleviate drought conditions in Burkina Faso, West Africa.

One of the most notable youth projects was in response to the war in the former Yugoslavia. One participant explains:

> *'In 1994 we sent a film crew to Mostar, Bosnia to film firsthand, while the war was still happening, how it was affecting the lives of children and young people there. The city was subject to constant shelling, had no constant water, electricity or food supplies. Sniper fire was a constant feature.*
>
> *We interviewed: kids who had seen their parents murdered, kidnapped, raped etc. Some kids had been raped themselves. Parents (mainly women, obviously) who were trying to make sense of the situation and provide for their kids, take care of elderly relatives and generally hold it all together.*
>
> *Although the racial tension in the city was tangible, in the midst of it the church was growing! Even when meetings were taking place the windows were being shot out by snipers (bit of a strange experience singing worship songs and hearing glass raining down the side of the building and thinking, "Er, those are real bullets . . . "), the rest of the congregation carried on singing so we figured we needed to do the same.*
>
> *We made a video that raised about £65,000 to support the work of two youth workers in Mostar. What we'd seen changed us and we knew that when we left the issues wouldn't go away, so we started a charity to provide ongoing support primarily for these two youth workers and the work they were doing.'*[122]

By 2000 the tradition of spreading justice through generosity was entrenched and Spring Harvest launched Generation 2000+, a week with a specific focus on family issues, in conjunction with Care for the Family.

Over £1.3 million was raised for needy children throughout the world through the 'Remember Me' offerings project, including a school offering project in Arusha, Tanzania. Here's an update on that project.

> *'The school started with only six students and now we have 32 students. Their ages are from fifteen to seventeen years (secondary age – form one which is equivalent to your year 9 in England). Please tell Spring Harvest that it was their first seed that helped us build the first two classrooms that are used now and from there we have added another two with toilet facilities and on top we will construct another three classrooms. So we really appreciate their support and prayers and please send our big thank you to them.'* [123]

The global coalition Stop the Traffik was launched at Spring Harvest in 2006 and has grown to become a force for change in the world with over 1000 Non Governmental Organizations (NGOs) as members worldwide. Even though it isn't technically a Spring Harvest charity, in 2007 Spring Harvest devoted the offerings project to raising awareness of human trafficking and raised over £1 million.

A force for change, Spring Harvest has started a tradition of launching, stimulating and supporting social justice initiatives from the UK to the whole world. Imagine what could be done if every person was convinced that the call to Christian discipleship was to impact the world for God? I'm convinced that the tradition set at this gathering is only the beginning . . . we are trusting God to awaken His church for His purposes. Contemporary William Booths, Elizabeth Frys and young potential William Wilberforces are hidden within the seats of auditoriums just moments away from world-changing behaviour – with earth-shaking results. Let this tradition stimulate, inspire and dare you to rise up and be the person God has called you to be – for the world's sake!

Community

A key to starting your journey is the understanding that social justice is not a lone ranger fight. In order to really fight injustice we need to do it in, through and with community. Christian community will always be God's preferred strategy to combat injustice.

We've attempted to arm you with some foundational truths – offering both the biblical tradition of justice and the foundations within the movement of the Christian church.

We've given you some specific tools to deal with injustice from both an international and local perspective – a prophetic response (engaging Scripture and the prophets), a systemic response (tools for unpacking the roots of oppression) and we've deliberately dealt with some of the practical politics of social justice to unpack the essentials.

We are calling you to *Just Imagine*. We wholeheartedly believe that the social justice fight can be engaged only with our imaginations aflame with justice. We want to be able to taste, smell and touch justice, to allow the familiarity with how things 'could' be to drive us to create a better world.

In the following section – Resources – we've provided you with a list of campaigns and movements emerging on the social justice scene that we can recommend, but there are many, many more. New initiatives are emerging every day and we encourage you to get informed and involved. It's time to live the dream.

Benediction

May the Lord disturb you and trouble you,
May the Lord set an impossible task before you,
And dare you to meet it.
May the Lord give you strength to do your best;
And then – but only then –
May the Lord grant you peace.

JUSTICE RESOURCES

The Micah Challenge (www.micahchallenge.org)
'Micah Challenge is a global Christian campaign. Our aims are to deepen our engagement with impoverished and marginalized communities; and to challenge international leaders, and leaders of rich and poor countries, to achieve the Millennium Development Goals, and so halve absolute global poverty by 2015!'

Make Poverty History (www.makepovertyhistory.org)
Make Poverty History is part of the Global Call to Action Against Poverty involving about 80 countries that aims to end the injustice of poverty. It is the largest anti-poverty movement in history.

Global Call to Action Against Poverty (www.whiteband.org)
The Global Call to Action against Poverty (GCAP) is a growing alliance of trade unions, community groups, faith groups, women and youth organizations, NGOs and other campaigners working together across more than 100 national platforms. GCAP is calling for action from the world's leaders to meet their promises to end poverty and inequality.

Stop The Traffik (www.stopthetraffik.org)
'Stop The Traffik is a global coalition of over 800 organizations in more than 50 countries working together in areas of advocacy, education and fundraising. Education: creating awareness and understanding of people trafficking. Advocacy: inspiring you to become an advocate for change, through getting involved and making a difference. Engaging with those who have the power to minimize the trafficking of people. Fundraising: financing anti-trafficking work around the world working with those vulnerable to and those who have been trafficked.'

ONE (www.one.org)
'As ONE, we are raising public awareness about the issues of global poverty, hunger, disease and efforts to fight such problems in the world's poorest countries. As ONE, we are asking our leaders to do more to fight the emergency of global AIDS and extreme poverty.'

Human Rights Watch (www.hrw.org)
'Human Rights Watch is dedicated to protecting the human rights of people around the world. We stand with victims and activists to prevent discrimination, to uphold political freedom, to protect people from inhumane conduct in wartime, and to bring offenders to justice. We investigate and expose human rights violations and hold abusers accountable. We challenge governments and those who hold power to end abusive practices and respect international human rights law. We enlist the public and the international community to support the cause of human rights for all.'

International Justice Mission (www.ijm.org)
IJM exists to protect people from violent forms of injustice by securing rescue and restoration for victims and accountability for perpetrators, ensuring that public justice systems work for the poor.

Fairtrade (www.fairtrade.org.uk)
'Our vision is of a world in which justice and sustainable development are at the heart of trade structures and practices so that everyone, through their work, can maintain a decent and dignified livelihood and develop their full potential. To achieve this vision, Fairtrade seeks to transform trading structures and practices in favour of the poor and disadvantaged. By facilitating trading partnerships based on equity and transparency, Fairtrade contributes to sustainable development for marginalized producers, workers and their communities. Through demonstration of alternatives to conventional trade and other forms of advocacy, the Fairtrade movement empowers citizens to campaign for an international trade system based on justice and fairness.'

Oxfam (www.oxfam.org)
'Oxfam International seeks increased worldwide public understanding that economic and social justice are crucial to sustainable development. We strive to be a global campaigning force promoting the awareness and motivation that comes with global citizenship while seeking to shift public opinion in order to make equity the same priority as economic growth. Key Campaigns: Make Trade Fair, Control Arms, Health & Education for All and Climate Change.'

Caritas Internationalis (www.caritas.org)
Caritas Internationalis is a confederation of 162 Catholic relief, development and social service organizations working to build a better world,

especially for the poor and oppressed, in over 200 countries and territories.

Bread for the World (www.bread.org)
'Bread for the World is a nationwide Christian movement that seeks justice for the world's hungry people by lobbying our nation's decision-makers.'

The Forgiveness Project (www.theforgivenessproject.com)
The Forgiveness Project is a charitable organization which explores forgiveness, reconciliation and conflict resolution through real-life human experience.

The Salvation Army (www.salvationarmy.org)
The Salvation Army is an integral part of the Christian church, although distinctive in government and practice. The Army's doctrine follows the mainstream of Christian belief and its articles of faith emphasise God's saving purposes. Its objects are 'the advancement of the Christian religion ... of education, the relief of poverty, and other charitable objects beneficial to society or the community of mankind as a whole.' The movement, founded in 1865 by William Booth, has spread from London, England, to many parts of the world. The website features the international mission and services of The Salvation Army, and provides links to the territorial headquarters which direct its work in over 119 countries.

Buy Nothing Day (www.buynothingday.co.uk)
'It's a day where you challenge yourself, your family and friends to switch off from shopping and tune into life. The rules are simple: for twenty-four hours you will detox from consumerism and live without shopping. Anyone can take part provided they spend a day without spending!'

Live Simply (www.livesimply.org.uk)
'The live simply project is based on a radical idea: that God calls us to live simply. We are asked to look hard at our lifestyles, and to choose to live simply, sustainably and in solidarity with the poor. It's not just about money. It's a challenge to reflect, celebrate and take action in order to work for justice, and to be happier in ourselves as a result. It's about seeking what we need rather than grasping for more, sharing not hoarding.'

Ash Barker, *Make Poverty Personal*, (Melbourne, UNOH, 2006)

BOOKS WE DIG ON JUSTICE

David Batstone, *Not For Sale: The Return of the Global Slave Trade and How We Can Fight It*, (London, HarperCollins, 2007)

Gary Bishop, *Darkest England and the Way Back In*, (Leicester, Matador, 2007)

Dietrich Bonhoeffer, *The Cost of Discipleship*, (London, SCM Press, 2001)

Dietrich Bonhoeffer, *Life Together*, (London, SCM Press, 1954)

Catherine Booth, *Aggressive Christianity*, (Plymouth, Diggory Press, 2005)

Wesley Campbell and Stephen Court, *Be A Hero: the Battle for Mercy and Social Justice*, (Shippensburg, Destiny Image, 2004)

Clayborne Carson (ed.), *The Autobiography of Martin Luther King, Jr.*, (New York, Warner Books, 2001)

Steve Chalke and Alan Mann, *The Lost Message of Jesus*, (Grand Rapids, Zondervan, 2003)

Shane Claiborne, *The Irresistible Revolution: Living as an Ordinary Radical*, (Grand Rapids, Zondervan, 2006)

Vincent J. Donovan, *Christianity Rediscovered*, (London, SCM Press, 2001)

Pete Greig and Dave Roberts, *Red Moon Rising: How 24-7 Prayer is Awakening a Generation*, (Eastbourne, Kingsway Publications, 2004)

Viv Grigg, *Cry of the Urban Poor*, (Milton Keynes, Authentic Media, 2005)

Ryszard Kapuscinski, *The Emperor*, (London, Penguin, 2006)

C. S. Lewis, *The Weight of Glory*, (London, Macmillan, 1949)

Nelson Mandela, *Long Walk to Freedom*, (London, Abacus, 1995)

Chris Marshall, *The Little Book of Biblical Justice*, (Good Books Publishing, 2006)

Nealson Munn and David Collinson, *Insane: the Stories of Crazy Salvos Who Changed the World*, (Australia, Salvo Publishing, 2007)

Ched Myers, Marie Dennis, Joseph Nangle OFM, Cynthia Moe-Lobeda and Stuart Taylor, *Say to This Mountain: Mark's story of discipleship,* (New York, Orbis Books, 1996)

Peggy Noonan, *John Paul the Great: Remembering a Spiritual Father*, (London, Penguin, 2006)

Muhammad Yunus, *Banker To The Poor*, (New York, Public Affairs, 1999)

Jeffrey Sachs, *The End of Poverty*, (London, Penguin, 2005)

Tom Sine, *The Mustard Seed Conspiracy*, (Christian Research, 1985)

Speeches That Changed the World, (London, Quercus, 2006)

Desmond Tutu, *No Future Without Forgiveness*, (New York, Doubleday, 1999)

Miroslav Volf, *Exclusion and Embrace*, (Nashville, Abingdon Press, 1994)

Jim Wallis, *God's Politics: Why the Right Gets It Wrong and the Left Doesn't Get It*, (Grand Rapids, Zondervan, 2005)

ENDNOTES

1 The spider is really a whole other story . . . Needless to say; it was as big as my hand and was very crunchy under my boot!

2 Prophetic judgment is a huge danger in the justice world. We can become adept at seeing the problems without offering any way out. This book is intended to help end that kind of justice rhetoric.

3 Check it out on YouTube or for a full transcript go to www.usconstitution.net/dream.html

4 Wesley Campbell and Stephen Court, *Be a Hero: the Battle for Mercy and Social Justice*, (Shippensburg, Destiny Image, 2004), p. 124

5 www.safecom.org.au/social-justice.htm

6 Read more on incarnation as a strategy for change in the story of Ashley Barker in *Surrender All: A Call to Sub-Merge with Christ*, or Viv Grigg's classic, *Cry of the Urban Poor.*

7 Clayborne Carson, ed., *The Autobiography of Martin Luther King, Jr.*, (New York, Warner Books, 2001) pp. 300-301

8 http://nobelprize.org/nobel_prizes/economics/laureates/1998/sen-autobio.html

9 Ched Myers, Marie Dennis, Joseph Nangle OFM, Cynthia Moe-Lobeda and Stuart Taylor, *Say to This Mountain: Mark's story of discipleship,* (New York, Orbis Books, 1996), p.xiii

10 Ash Barker, *Make Poverty Personal* (Melbourne, UNOH, 2006), p. 11. We highly recommend this book to learn more about the Bible's call to end oppression.

11 The larger portion of scripture is helpful to read for full context: Exodus 22:16-31.

12 Chris Marshall, *The Little Book of Biblical Justice*, (Good Books, 2005)

13 Brad Jersak, *Can you hear me?* (Toronto, Monarch Books, 2006) pp. 220-221

14 http://web.princeton.edu/sites/chapel/Sermon%20Files/2004_sermons/030704.htm

15 Brad Jersak, *Can You Hear Me?* p. 229

16 Go to www.sojo.net/index.cfm?action=magazine.article&issue=soj9807&article=980724 for the full article.

17 For more information see www.elizabethfry.ca

18 Campbell and Court, *Be a Hero*

19 Roger J. Green, *The Life and Ministry of William Booth: Founder of the Salvation Army*, (Nashville, Abingdon Press, 2006)

20 Harold Begbie, *The Life of General William Booth: The Founder of the Salvation Army*, (London, Macmillan, 1920) p. 249

21 Roger J. Green, *The Life and Ministry of William Booth*, p. 173

22 Roger J. Green, *The Life and Ministry of William Booth*, p. 173

23 William Booth, *In Darkest England and the Way Out*, (Montana, Kessinger Publishing, 2004) p. 33

24 Roger J. Green, *The Life and Ministry of William Booth*, p. 198

25 Harold Begbie, *The Life of General William Booth*

26 Nealson Munn and David Collinson, *Insane: Stories of Crazy Salvos Who Changed the World*, (Australia, Salvo Publishing, 2007) p. 111

27 Munn and Collinson, *Insane*, p. 62

28 We highly recommend getting hold of a copy of *Insane* to read the full account!

29 The Cab Horse Charter shamed the public and galvanized support for his immense project. Booth followed this up with a well-publicized success to demonstrate the viability of the plan. He tackled and transformed the match industry in England. See Campbell and Court, *Be a Hero.*

30 www.youtube.com/watch?v=rvTFKpIaQhM&feature=related

31 Australian Catholic Social Justice Council, Social Justice Sunday Statement for 2007, *Who is my Neighbour? Australia's role as a global citizen,* p.3

32 Mother Teresa, *Words to Love By*, (Notre Dame, Ave Maria Press, 1985) p. 79

33 http://news.bbc.co.uk/1/hi/uk_politics/4232603.stm

34 www.sfu.ca/~oxfam/archive.htm

35 World Bank, 2006 World Development Indicators – Regional Poverty Estimates

36 http://nobelprize.org/nobel_prizes/peace/laureates/2006/yunus-lecture-en.html

37 Read more about Fairtrade at www.fairtrade.org.uk

38 Australian Catholic Social Justice Council, Social Justice Sunday Statement for 2007, *Who is my Neighbour? Australia's role as a global citizen*, p. 6

39 Maurice Strong, facilitator of the Earth Summit.

40 Millennium Goals www.unmillenniumproject.org/goals/index.htm

41 World Bank, 2006, Clean Energy and Development: Towards an Investment Framework, Environmentally and Socially Sustainable Development Vice Presidency

42 Oxfam currently has a campaign called 'Fight Climate Poverty'. See their website for more details: www.oxfam.org.uk/applications/climate/index.php/Register.html

43 World Bank, 2006, Clean Energy and Development

44 Desmond Tutu, *No Future Without Forgiveness*, (New York, Doubleday, 1999) pp. 217-218

45 Check out www.beahero.org or www.armybarmy.com/be-a-hero.html

46 The Emet System is a concept that comes from a French psychotherapist and management school. This approach develops some ideas of Jacques Lacan. According to the System, the only person perfectly harmonized is Jesus.

47 http://usliberals.about.com/od/faithinpubliclife/a/BonoSermon_3.htm

48 Peter Hosking, *Introduction to Social Justice and Social Analysis*, (Jesuit Social Justice Centre, www.uniya.org/publications/pdfs/o_social_justice.pdf) p. 6

49 Peter Singer, *One World: the Ethics of Globalization,* (New Haven, Yale University Press, 2002) p. 189

50 Chad Myers explains, 'The theology of Sabbath economics and its ethic of regular and systemic wealth and power redistribution - most clearly summed up in the Jubilee release of slaves, deconstruction of debt and return of foreclosed land - is neither utopian nor abstract. It arose out of the concrete Hebrew experience of slavery in Egypt, and so is both corrective and preventative. I

believe it continues to offer communities of faith today a way out of our historical and persistent slavery to the debt system, with its competing theology of meritocracy and its alienating and cruel practices of wealth and power concentration and social stratification.' www.earthministry.org/3e/pmap/sabbath.htm

51 www.sojo.net/index.cfm?action=magazine.article&issue=soj9807&article=980724

52 www.wakethesleepinggiant.info/faqs.html

53 Shane Claiborne, *The Irresistible Revolution: Living as an Ordinary Radical* (Grand Rapids, Zondervan, 2006) p. 165

54 Jan Nederveen-Pieterse and Sabina Alkire, 2002 in Fantu Cheru and Colin Bradford (eds.), *The Millennium Development Goals: Raising the resources to tackle world poverty*, (London, Zed Books Ltd, 2005) p.11

55 www.uri.edu/artsci/wms/hughes/demand_sex_trafficking.pdf

56 Article 3 of the Protocol to Prevent, Suppress and Punish Trafficking in Persons, Especially Women and Children, Supplementing the United Nations Convention Against Transnational Organised Crime (Palmero Protocol)

57 'A Global Alliance Against Forced Labor', International Labour Organization, 2005

58 US Department of State Trafficking in Persons Report 2005

59 UNICEF UK Child Trafficking Information sheet, January 2003

60 'A Global Alliance Against Forced Labor', International Labour Organization, 2005

61 UN Office on Drugs and Crime

62 UN Office on Drugs and Crime

63 atheism.about.com/od/popejohnpaulii/a/capitalism.htm

64 Victor Malarek, *The Natashas*, (New York, Arcade Publishing, 2004) p. 128

65 Peter Singer, *One World: the Ethics of Globalization*, pp. 167-168

66 Tony Campolo and Gordon Aeschliman, *Everybody Wants to Change the World: Practical Ideas for Social Justice* (Ventura, Regal, 2006) p. 108

67 www.uri.edu/artsci/wms/hughes/demand_sex_trafficking.pdf

68 Victor Malarek, *The Natashas*

69 Campolo and Aeschliman, *Everybody Wants to Change the World*, p. 109

70 http://216.128.18.195/IJMpdfs/070322_HollyTestifiesBeforeSenateSubcommittee.pdf

71 Victor Malarek, *The Natashas*, p. 119

72 www.uri.edu/artsci/wms/hughes/demand_sex_trafficking.pdf

73 www.stopthetraffik.org

74 www.theccat.com

75 This was an important focus for Muhammad Yunus as he established the Grameen Bank. He found women lacked basic rights and freedom to access paid employment. By lending them capital they could work themselves out of their own poverty. Empowering them became a strategy for alleviating poverty in the country. 'It is believed that 25 million people worldwide are now using microcredit to undertake income-generating or self-employment activities; of these, 90 per cent are women. Microcredit has not only made women more productive, it has also empowered them. As a result women are now integrated into socio-economic activities, contributing to family income and decision making and exercising more control over their fertility, which allows them to take better care of their children.' (Kaniz Fahmida Ahmed, *Microcredit as a Tool for Women Empowerment: The Case of Bangladesh*, www.foreignaid.com/thinktank/microcredit.html)

76 Sometimes the church has not been helpful to this cause. The worse offenders often use the Bible to promote inequality and gender discrimination. However, a thorough examination of scripture will inevitably lead to the promotion of women's rights.

77 'Pornography and sexual violence; the connection has been made that when we objectify another person's gender, we leave that person open to pure utilization. The humanity of the person disappears when we perceive him or her simply through our personal sense of pleasure or gratification. Women's bodies ultimately finance the pornography industry that generates billions of dollars in revenue annually. But at what cost to their bodies?' Campolo and Aeschliman, *Everybody Wants to Change the World*, p. 103

78 For example, in many Western countries there are some grave human rights violations with regards to immigration in the policies that are responsible for creating detainment centres.

79 Muhammad Yunus uses this term to explain what he did in order to understand oppression in Bangladesh.

80 For the full speech go to www.one.org/blog/2007/03/06/bonos-acceptance-speech/

81 For the full speech go to nobelprize.org/nobel_prizes/peace/laureates/2006/yunus-lecture-en.html

82 http://blog.case.edu/singham/2005/12/05/hotel_rwanda_and_postcolonial_ethnic_conflicts

83 Ekberg advocated a three-pronged approach: decriminalizing of prostitutes, criminalizing of 'johns', and major funding for exit programs to re-enter women into society. Go to http://action.web.ca/home/catw/attach/Ekberg.pdf

84 Muhammad Yunus, *Banker to the Poor*, (New York, Public Affairs, 1999) p. 23

85 Check out the whole story in Munn and Collinson, *Insane*, chapter four: 'The Maiden Tribute of Modern Babylon'.

86 Rebecca Jerritt received a sentence of six months, Stead three months and Booth was acquitted.

87 For the full Nobel Peace Prize Speech go to http://nobelprize.org/nobel_prizes/peace/laureates/2006/yunus-lecture-en.html

88 For more information on the Grameen Bank go to http://www.grameen-info.org/

89 R.T. Kendall, *Total Forgiveness: Achieving God's Greatest Challenge,* (London, Hodder & Stoughton, 2003) p. ix

90 R.T. Kendall, *Total Forgiveness*, p. xii

91 R.T. Kendall, *Total Forgiveness*, p. xii

92 Brad Jersak, *Can you hear me?* p. 221

93 Walter Brueggemann, *The Prophetic Imagination*, (Minneapolis, Augsburg Fortress, 2001) p. 2

94 From the album *Heart Life Voice* by Micah Challenge http://www.heartlifevoice.org/

95 Eric Metaxas, *Amazing Grace: William Wilberforce and the Heroic Campaign to End Slavery*, (New York, HarperOne, 2007) p. xv

96 Incarnational monastic communities are a new prophetic breed of people choosing to join existing economically-challenged neighbourhoods in order to bring the Kingdom close.

97 The Salvation Army International Health Services, *Strategies and Tools for Integrated Mission-Influencing Policy*

98 The Salvation Army International Health Services, *Strategies and Tools*

99 You can find out more about the Booth–Tucker Institute at www.thewarcollege.com/bti_info.html

100 The Five Principles are from Robert McAfee Brown, *Theology in a New Key, Responding to Liberation Themes*, (Philadelphia, Westminster Press, 1978). We have included them as a tool for analysing context.

101 Rob Bell, *Sex God: Exploring the Endless Connections Between Sexuality and Spirituality*, (Grand Rapids, Zondervan, 2007) p. 15

102 Although this is true in some countries, we also recognize some governments' clear bias against those who speak up politically. The funding reality can be a valid issue which we need to grapple with but certainly not shy away from.

103 There has been a lot of controversy surrounding China's hosting of the 2008 Olympic Games. For more information see http://china.hrw.org/

104 http://en.wikipedia.org/wiki/First_they_came...

105 Some Christian organizations have discussion guides for elections to help aid people in critical thought and debate regarding political discussions – these are new innovations to re-engage in political justice.

106 Recognizing that the political arena can be a difficult place, it is particularly important for the church to create meaningful and direct relationship-based support and mentoring.

107 http://kellogg.nd.edu/romero/pdfs/Biography.pdf

108 Walter Brueggemann, *The Prophetic Imagination*

109 There is a great new resource available called *Living Simply: Studies in Learning to Live As Jesus Did*, by Murray Sheard, released by Tearfund and World Vision. You can email msheard@auckland.ac.nz to order a copy.

110 Extravagant generosity is the basic level for the New Testament church on giving. Our typical ten per cent variety of tithing is at best a poor reflection of basic biblical stewardship.

111 'It's a day where you challenge yourself, your family and friends to switch off from shopping and tune into life. The rules are simple,

for 24 hours you will detox from consumerism and live without shopping.' For more information see www.buynothingday.co.uk.

112 There are many incarnational communities who have agreed lifestyle commitments. These include individual and communal commitments. Urban Neighbours of Hope (UNOH) are one such community. Commitments include practical response such as 'Hospitality', 'Voluntary Poverty', 'Just Stewardship' & 'Servanthood'. Check out www.unoh.org for more information.

113 www.relationaltithe.com

114 For example, as a church or small group you could sponsor a micro-finance trust bank which empowers women in the developing world. For more information on how to do this, see www.justsalvos.com/justgifts/index.php?content=14

115 www.amnesty.org

116 www.stopthetraffik.org

117 www.greenpeace.org

118 At the 2002 Monterrey Conference, leaders of the world's wealthiest countries reaffirmed their commitment to the UN target of 0.7 per cent ratio of Official Development Assistance (aid to the poorest countries) to Gross National Income. To date, most countries are still far behind this target. In 2006, in comparison to Sweden's impressive 1.02 per cent, Australia was at 0.30, New Zealand 0.27, Canada 0.29, United States 0.18, United Kingdom 0.51, and Japan 0.25. www.un.org/esa/sustdev/documents/Monterrey_Consensus.htm and the Organization for Economic Co-operation and Development www.oecd.org/dataoecd/7/20/39768315.pdf

119 Claiborne, *Irresistible Revolution*, pp. 128-129

120 Campbell and Court, *Be a Hero*, p. 223

121 For a detailed timeline check out www.springharvest.org/about-us-sh/history-sh/module_index.php?id=1

122 The charity is still going. There is no official link to Spring Harvest, but you'll see what they do at www.novimost.org

123 http://www.newlifeband.net/documents/38.html